Being a WILD, Wonderful Woman for God

Being a WILD, Wonderful Woman for God

Becky Tirabassi

ZondervanPublishingHouse

Grand Rapids, Michigan

A Division of HarperCollinsPublishers

Requests for information should be addressed to:
  Zondervan Publishing House
  Grand Rapids, MI   49530

Library of Congress Cataloging-in-Publication Data

Tirabassi, Becky, 1954–
      Being a wild wonderful woman for God / Becky Tirabassi
          p. cm.
      ISBN 0-310-44250-8
          1. Tirabassi, Becky, 1954–   . 2. Christian biography—United
States. 3. Adult children of dysfunctional families—United States—
Biography. 4. Women—Religious life. I. Title.
BR1725.T57A3   1994
248.8'092—dc20
[B]
94-26655
                                                                          CIP

Cover design by Cheryl Van Andel
Cover photography by David Winterhalter
Interior design by Sherri L. Hoffman

Printed in the United States of America

94 95 96 97 98 99 00 01 02 03 /❖ DH / 10 9 8 7 6 5 4 3 2 1

This edition is printed on acid-free paper and meets the American National
Standards Institute Z39.48 standard.

Contents

Foreword:
A New Generation

A new generation of women is emerging in America today. We are neither radical feminists nor fundamentalists. We are unlike the generations of women who have gone before us. We defy the stereotypes.

We are women who have been through the most difficult of times, including recovery from drugs, alcohol, and sexual and physical abuses—even at the hands of those we have loved.

We are women who have made our own spiritual pilgrimages. Many of us have had to find faith on our own, and we are still on a journey of discovering a new and more lasting spirituality.

We live with a host of overwhelming expectations. Often by necessity, many of us are mothers *and* working women. Some manage to combine being board members and food-pantry volunteers; some work as computer operators and still serve as round-the-clock taxi services for their kids. Yet we are strong and courageous, full of hope and integrity.

With one loud voice we are saying, "We can't turn the clock back, so whom can we be today?" We are struggling to find our balance. We are trying to pinpoint who speaks for us.

We have emerged into the nineties as wild, wonderful women for God.

This is *our* story . . .

Being a *WILD,* Wonderful Woman for God

Chapter One

The Dysfunctional Dynasty

*M*any of us started our life journey in dysfunctional families. Love—in the form of kisses, hugs, nurturing, sacrifice, financial provision, understanding, gentle discipline, mutual respect, and responsible freedoms—was put on the back burner for those of us who grew up in these homes. Instead, we experienced rage, abuse, and disillusionment. Both the children and the adults inside these homes were desperate for life to make sense, while on the outside they played the All-American, church-going, traditional family roles.

My own family played out this dysfunctional nightmare in our home, until my older sister went off to college and my older brother went off to serve in the Air Force during the Vietnam war in 1968. As the last of the children in our home, I battled my way through junior high and high school with a non-violent, but alcoholic father and an angry, disillusioned-with-her-life but very independent, controlling mother.

Before my sophomore year in high school, my father had a stroke resulting from alcohol and cigarette abuse, as well as severe high blood pressure. He was partially disabled, and he retired early from his job as a quality-control manager. In addition, my dad's sister, Aunt Mary Jane, was already living in our home. She had trouble speaking and walked with a cane because of an aneurysm she had suffered at the age of forty-three due to an overdose of alcohol and drugs. (Even my dad's father had suffered with alcoholism until his early death.)

Oddly, the high number of alcoholics in my family did not stop me from drinking. And since my whole family scene was embarrassing to me, I never told others of my shame, nor did I ever fully understand the dysfunction and inherited traits of which I was an unknowing victim. Because my family could still function on certain levels (my dad went to work every day, and we all went to church on Sundays), I actually thought that our home life was fairly normal. I just didn't want to spend a lot of time there.

The only way I could make myself happy was to party. Drinking was a socially acceptable way for a teenager to be liberated from a fragmented home life, rejoice in the ecstasy of escapism, and tackle the adventures of school, sexuality, and independence with a wild-eyed freedom. Because my personality leaned toward having fun, and I obviously had a great need to be loved and accepted, I proceeded to drink hard enough to diminish my sexual inhibitions. I became both the "life of the party" *and* an alcoholic by the age of sixteen.

Just try to tell a teenager who loves life and laughter, music and dancing and fun, that the horrors of home are not worth rebelling against and running away from. Try to tell her that drugs and alcohol and sexual experiences won't make the bad things go away. Try to convince her that getting "high" won't necessarily make her *feel* any better. Or try to tell a love-hungry young woman that sex doesn't equal love *or* that living with someone doesn't always mean that he wants to marry you! She won't believe you. Or she just won't care.

You won't easily convince her because often that young woman finds drugs, alcohol, sex, and her partying friends to be her greatest resources of love and happiness. In fact, the partying crowd becomes her extended family. And even though this love is often fickle and elusive, it temporarily satisfies her love hunger.

It took me another six years of drinking, followed by almost fifteen years of sobriety before I understood that much of my search for acceptance and love as a young woman was a refocusing of unmet childhood needs.

Millions of women now in their thirties and forties have grown up in emotionally, physically, or sexually abusive families. At my speaking engagements, I've spoken to thousands of women, and hundreds have come up to say, "You have just told my story." Bonding like sisters, we agreed that our radical attempts to cope with the breakdown of our families—through our own choices of rebelliousness, addiction, and sexual experimentation—though unsuccessful, were extremely different pathways than the compliant, even passive, generations before us.

Not until the summer of 1992 did I reach the end of *my* elusive search for love and self-acceptance. That year I celebrated my sixteenth spiritual birthday, and my sixteenth year of sobriety. On August 26, 1976, I became a Christian, and decided to stop drinking. The direction of my life changed like a weather vane blown from north to south by one abrupt gust.

But as I said, the fulfillment of this change in direction took a long time. In the spring of 1992, I trained to become a small group leader in a Twelve Step Group for students. Part of the training included walking through the Twelve Steps myself with an intimate group of four other adults. I had received varying degrees of support from friends and groups during the previous sixteen years, but I had never been a member of an actual Twelve Step Group. Initially, I avoided Twelve Step meetings because during the 1970s groups such as AA were not necessarily geared for young people—or not the ones I attended, at least. The first time I, as a twenty-one-year-old woman, attended a meeting, I walked into a roomful of men in their forties. We all felt awkward with our obvious age and gender differences—and because of that, I never felt comfortable enough to go back.

Therefore, not until my late thirties, after I had volunteered with kids and spoken to adults and students nationwide on my alcoholism, did I get involved in the Twelve Steps. My greatest motivation for becoming a small group leader was to "be there" for *kids* who needed and wanted to talk about their addictions, problems, fears, and angers. But the most interesting outcome of my training was my own personal healing and the incredible self-revelations I experienced.

Through each of the Twelve Steps—which include forgiveness, making amends to people you have hurt, and taking your personal inventory—I began to relive the pain and rejection of being a sixteen-year-old girl who lacked paternal nurturing. My father never encouraged my tender femininity with those important gestures by which fathers guide their daughters through the unwritten rites of passage to womanhood. My parents never gave me a strand of pearls, a rose, a ring, or a card. They did not allow me to take social dance classes, have my ears pierced, or go to college (unless I paid for it). I acknowledged these disappointments; my heart ached. I realized that in covering up the pain of those losses for all of these years, I had grown bitter and resentful toward my parents.

Those honest reflections led me to see why I became the kind of girl boys didn't ask to the prom—but the kind of girl they went drinking with.

As an adult woman, I felt very sad for that young sixteen-year-old girl. . . .

At that point in our training, we were asked to read a portion of the Bible: Joel 2 from the Old Testament Prophets. While doing my homework, I stopped at a particular verse: "I will repay you for the years the locusts have eaten." I believed God used this verse to encourage me!

At the next weekly meeting, we were asked to share what the Joel verses had meant to each of us. When it was my turn, I leaned forward, and hesitantly, quietly, I described the vivid memories of my teenage years that these verses had elicited. Tears in my eyes, I said, "I believe that God really loves me, that he sees me as his beautiful, young daughter, and because my sixteenth spiritual and sobriety birthdays are coming up, I believe he's going to give me a very special birthday present." The members of my small group all looked at me, nodding their heads. (The greatest thing about a Twelve Step Group is that the members do not give you advice, but only encouragement and support.)

Later that night, as I remembered each of their comments and prayers, I felt added assurance and hope that God was indeed going to give me a special birthday present on August 26. But because this idea sounded far out, I didn't tell anyone else—not even my husband.

Over the next few months that verse in Joel, "I will repay you for the years the locusts have eaten . . ." began to heal my heart and mind and memories.

I knew that I have a heavenly Father who really loves me—and he can show me just how much he loves me. He is perfect in his ability to love me, he is not afraid to spoil me or withhold something from me, and he is not ashamed of me. Nor is he dysfunctional. He is a most loving, approving, and even doting Father. He is not like my earthly father.

The sheer realization that I was so loved by and so special to my Heavenly Father made me contemplate just how much love I must have missed by running so hard from him during my teenage years! Those thoughts ultimately gave me a new understanding and deep compassion for my earthly parents.

The Big Day

On Friday, August 25, 1992, my husband Roger reminded me that we were going to a Jazz Festival at the Hyatt Newporter with a group of friends. I was looking forward to a really fun night. As we were walking out our front door, I said to Roger, "You're going to be leaving for a trip to Canada tomorrow, and you won't be here to celebrate my sixteenth spiritual birthday." He acknowledged my remark with a "Uh-huh" and a nod.

We walked up to the second floor of the hotel to meet our friends in the hotel pre-jazz festival suite. When I opened the door, the first thing I saw was streamers and balloons, and a banner that said "HAPPY SIXTEENTH BIRTHDAY!" A roomful of friends yelled, "Surprise!"

I was speechless! I turned to see if there was a sixteen-year-old girl coming in the door behind me. No, this party was for me. Roger had not forgotten my sixteenth spiritual and sobriety birthdays.

Soon Roger said that we needed to claim our front-row seats down on the lawn of the hotel for the festival. Almost as quickly as we had entered the room, we headed down the stairs.

Roger led me through the lobby of the hotel and out into the valet parking area. Before I could say, "This isn't the way to the Jazz Festival," I looked up to find all my friends, who had just been in the hotel suite with me, now surrounding a little red convertible with a huge red bow on it! On the windshield of this little convertible was another "HAPPY SIXTEENTH BIRTHDAY" banner! Again, I turned around to see if I were sharing this special night with someone else.

My thoughts raced from the verse in Joel 2 to the dream I had shared only with my small support group—that God was going to give me a very special birthday present. In that fleeting moment, I realized that the most awesome birthday gift any sixteen-year-old girl could ever want would be a very cool, red convertible.

I was struck with the significance of a car as the gift my husband would choose for my sixteenth spiritual birthday! I couldn't get over the surprise of it all—my husband has never even had a surprise party for me on my real birthday, and our practice in exchanging gifts has always been to give gifts that were either small or simple. Even more unusual was the fact that I hadn't asked for or even so much as hinted at wanting or needing a car!

To make the evening more unbelievable, I had not told the "Joel 2" story to my husband. God must have orchestrated this event himself by putting this idea in my husband's heart and mind. What other explanation could there be?

As we got into bed that night, my husband confessed his exhaustion. He described to me how agonizing it was to keep this secret, how difficult it was to sell another person's car, and how nerve-wracking it was to choose and purchase another one! For days he worried, "Would I like it? Would I find out? Would someone spoil the surprise?" Not to worry, I applauded him!

The following week I had a strong inner sense that God had seen my love hunger all of these years, that he had cried with me when I had cried. I knew he had seen my wild dashes for attention, affection, affirmation, and approval. He had seen how often I had humiliated myself. Somehow that little party gave me the impression that God had been aware that I had, sixteen years earlier, courageously given up my patterns of looking for love in all the wrong places and found the love of my heavenly Father just waiting for me. He had proven to me convincingly that if I would just daily hold his hand and walk with him, I *would* forever have a true love—accepting and unconditional.

Being loved when you haven't earned it holds an incredible potential for healing in one's life. By understanding God's forgiveness we can finally forgive ourselves and those who have hurt us. No longer did I have to hunger for my parents' love and approval. I now felt free to *love them* unconditionally.

God had shown me that I am loved today with more love than I could ever need or desire. At last, I could finally let go of trying to remake my past or make up for the way my childhood should or could have been. It was time to move on, to forgive, to rejoice, to feel special, and to love!

Begin at the Beginning

To pursue reconciliation and forgiveness within one's own family is every woman's beginning place. When we can resolve conflicts and make restitution for past mistakes in our relationships, the relief and release that this forgiveness brings allows us to go on with a fulfilling new life.

Though our search for love may have been a continuous battle, that struggle loses its power over us when we accept the past, forgive those who have offended us, and realize just how much we have *now*, rather than dwelling upon what we have missed. When we focus on the current, positive aspects of our lives, whether it is our understanding spouse, healthy children, or the genuine closeness with a special family or group of friends, we are free to allow those relationships to fill voids and replace the emptiness of the past.

You're Not Alone

Many women—and the statistics are horrendous—have been abused, neglected, and rejected at birth, in childhood, as teenagers, or as young women. We may be one of the most dysfunctional generations of women in the history of America.

But in America today a woman does not need to fall prey to depression, addiction, or victimization. Many have stepped through the doors to healing. We've begun with tears that only hint at our inexpressible pain, and then we cry out for help from a friend, even a stranger, who encourages us to hope once again, live once again, even love once again.

Many of my friends have suffered from abusive relationships, been addicted to substances, or been divorced. Yet, by seeking help in support groups, Bible studies, and Twelve Step groups, they are courageously working through their problems, addictions, and failures, rather than running from them.

Women in America no longer have to sit back and waste away, to live life only with regrets, fears, anger, and unforgiveness. Rather, we can opt for a new life, a fresh start, a second chance.

It's not easy. It takes courage. Recently, my twenty-three-year-old friend Carol identified and admitted her eating disorder. How painful it was for her to acknowledge that she was chained to such self-destructive patterns. She took a leave of absence from her job, entered a treatment center, and began the process of healing that comes with both the daily renewal of the Holy Spirit and by surrounding herself with the support of healthy, mature Christians.

Many women write to me or talk with me after speaking engagements who touch my life with their stories of addiction or betrayal. Each one details her own path to reconciliation, restoration, and recovery. They are the wives of workaholic pastors, the spouses of homosexual husbands, the children of abusive parents or husbands. And in many instances they have overcome.

We are women who are no longer at an impasse. We are no longer threatened or discouraged. Instead, we have discovered that admitting our weaknesses and our need for God's help is the beginning of personal growth! We are free to create a new heritage for our family and to develop new habits and traditions to pass along to them. We are making new memories for our children to have and hold on to later in *their* lives. It has been worth the hard emotional work to find healing.

We are learning to forgive. We are learning to love.

Although our stories started in dysfunctional families, we choose to live in the solution. We no longer define ourselves in terms of our problems, but in the healthy lives we now lead.

But first we need to confront our own sexuality.

Chapter Two

Doesn't Sex Equal Love?

At nineteen, I dropped out of Bowling Green State University, moved to California, and felt independent enough to live with my boyfriend—I'll call him "Danny." Though I had been raised to believe that you only live together if married, I was easily swayed to think a "live-in" lifestyle was acceptable because "everyone was doing it." I continued to buy into the philosophy epitomized in the seventies that sex equaled love.

By age twenty, I also thought that if a man wanted to live with me, he would also want to marry me—eventually. Besides, at that age, living together seemed more romantic than marriage. I slipped into the trap of being a sexual partner without any promise of long-term emotional or relational commitment.

My thoughts on procreation were shallow: Like so many other young, unwed live-in partners, I felt if I *did* get pregnant

21

—inconveniently—I could easily get an abortion. This option allowed me to be carefree and careless about birth control, knowing that, if I had to, I could quickly get rid of any unwanted encumbrance.

But was that what I really wanted? Only now can I be brutally honest with myself. As I examine my motives in neglecting to use birth control, I have to admit that perhaps I was hoping to become pregnant, not only to have a child, but to force a commitment from this man. I must also confess that it was simply by the grace of God that I had not gotten pregnant during that promiscuous stage of my life. (From the first day of my only marriage, and for the last sixteen years, except when my husband and I were trying to conceive, not one single day has gone by that I have forgotten to use birth control. If you don't want to get pregnant, you don't "forget.")

I can only presume that my search for love back in those early days, as well as my misconception that sex equaled love, was powerful enough to drive me to give more of myself to someone than I wanted to. My illusion that sex would be a lasting bond between two unmarried, uncommitted young people proved devastating.

Daily I lived in a *constant* state of insecurity and guilt. Each morning and evening I would numb myself with speed and alcohol. Not a day went by when I didn't feel ashamed to tell the people at work that I was living with my boyfriend, and, of course, I couldn't tell my parents who my roommate was. But I kept giving in sexually—often against my own desires—even when I was being made to do things I didn't want to do. (Perhaps I thought it was the only way that I could "keep" this guy?) Danny made no promises to me, but he had many expectations.

Our relationship seemed to waiver between his demand for freedom and my demand for commitment. Though I never worried that he would find someone new, I was always concerned that Danny would return to a *former* live-in girlfriend—of which he had several over the previous five years. It became my daily obsession to find out if he had remained faithful to me.

I agonized over in-coming calls from girls I didn't know. Were they from his past? I questioned his "out of town" camping and business trips, always suspecting that he might have an intimate rendezvous planned.

Yet I put up with the suspense and uncertainty simply because I had no other choice—unless, of course, I wanted to move out, give him an ultimatum, and possibly lose him. The power that this relationship had over me stemmed from my belief that I *needed* him to be happy. I felt sure Danny was the man I would marry, but every discussion about marriage and a life-long commitment ended the same way: Danny "just wasn't ready." At twenty-six years old, he was "too young." Instead, we played house. He kept the door wide open to walk out, and I clung to his pant leg every time he moved or even glanced toward the door.

Oddly, other men were interested in dating me, but I stoically proclaimed my loyalty to my live-in boyfriend. For a long time, even when I went on drunken binges and was propositioned, I would refuse others' advances. I felt adamant about maintaining at least my half of the relationship.

And yet, the final, crushing blow to this morally loose lifestyle was an escapade where *I* became the one who could not be trusted when drinking.

Our plan was to go separate ways for a long summer vacation. I wouldn't have to worry about his faithfulness, I told myself, because Danny would be on a camping trip. I was on my way home to Ohio to be in a wedding.

But even as Danny drove me to the airport, I was afraid to let him go. I sobbed uncontrollably, afraid that our relationship might never be the same, almost projecting his unfaithfulness as imminent. Inside, I was emotionally drained from distrust and from hating myself for being so dependent on him.

But consuming enough liquor—from the moment I boarded the airplane until I began to party every waking minute away with old friends—temporarily subdued the fear of rejection and the pain of loneliness.

By Thursday night at the bachelorette party, I was in rare form. Without hesitation, I drank half of a fifth of vodka and drove my friends to the local bar to drink and dance. How I spent the next hours are still uncertain, but eventually I lost my friends, left my car, and awoke at 6:00 in the morning next to someone I barely knew. For the very first time I really understood how uncontrollable sex outside of marriage could be. I was convinced beyond doubt that alcohol has no regard for one's deepest commitments. My first sober thoughts were, "Becky, do you know what you call girls like this? . . . You would *never* have done this if you hadn't been drinking."

I have never felt more disgusted with myself. I knew this was not freedom. This was not a fun fling. This was a life out of control. This was a woman being used—and using others— while under the influence of a judgment-blurring drug. Even the powerful force of my love for my boyfriend was not stronger than the alcohol in my system.

In the end, I was the one who was promiscuous. That humiliating experience was the beginning of the end of that lifestyle for me. Though many women deal with sexual addiction and dependency, when my *drinking* stopped, my actions and judgments about sexual intimacy and morality completely reversed. When sober, I had cautious inhibition. I recognized, without being told, that sexual intimacy without the promises made in marriage only breeds insecurity, doubt, mistrust, and promiscuity.

What I needed—and wanted—in a relationship was security, self-respect, and boundaries. Finally, at twenty-one, with the help of God, I made an abrupt (some have even called it miraculous) 180-degree lifestyle change to reach for emotional and physical stability. I became a Christian and resolved to live in the light of the truth I had found. My resolves, however, did not signal the end of my relationship with Danny. I just wanted to stop the sexual part of it—*until* we got married. For my own sanity, one August day, I decided to abstain from sex until marriage, so I moved out of our home. Saying "no" to Danny—or any other man—was a choice I made out of respect for myself.

Optimistically, I had every expectation that we would still get married and that he would respect my new-found faith. I was hopeful that our love would only deepen.

Every day Danny would come over to my apartment after work, help make dinner, and attempt to rekindle our previously affectionate and intimate relationship.

He would hug and kiss me. I would back away, talk about God, and energetically engage in a discussion about the beauty of married sexuality spoken of in the Bible. He grew angry and resentful of my newfound faith.

Sometimes he would leave early. Other nights he would lure me over to the couch. But *every* night, I determined I would not do two things with him: drink or have sex.

Because of my convictions, I was now becoming a woman of strength, rather than one who just months earlier had been pathetically weak. And though it wasn't easy, my new-found strength came from the principles of love, sex, and marriage set forth in the Bible—of which I had become a new student. Those teachings offered me guidelines with promises. They offered boundaries that had *my* best interests at heart! They restored my self-respect. I was exhilarated by the whole idea of saving the sexual part of our relationship until marriage!

I wanted to experience a safe and secure sexual relationship! I began to dream about marriage, looking forward to going to bed at night with Danny *and not* having a huge presence of guilt over me. I grew eager to be respected (rather than embarrassed) by my co-workers and friends because of a marriage vow that Danny and I would make in front of God and others to live together forever! I felt that a marriage proposal would signify how deeply committed Danny was to me.

But Danny didn't think these new boundaries or marital commitments were wonderful at all. He felt they were outdated. Initially, he tolerated my beliefs, but as time went by, it became obvious that he fully expected me to give in to our previous patterns of sexual intimacy—as I had done so many times before.

Then came a tearful discussion, after a candlelight dinner, between two people who had once known and loved each other, but had finally come to an impasse over God and sex. We slipped from the table and snuggled together in a bean-bag chair on the floor. His strong arms were wrapped around my shoulders in a protective, possessive manner. In the same moment, I felt both a physical closeness and an emotional, perhaps even spiritual, distance.

Our often repeated discussion began once again. . . .

"Becky, this abstinence stuff is crazy. It's old-fashioned. It's not how to show someone you love them. It's hurting us, driving a wedge between us . . ." Danny said this so convincingly. He was so *sure* that he was right.

"But I can't. I've decided not to have sex with a man until we're married," I replied with as much confidence as he had, but with much more sadness.

The distance between us kept growing. He was telling me he would not come my way. . . .

"Becky, God is for weak people who need a crutch. I'm not weak. Neither are you. You don't need God to control your life. You're not an alcoholic. You just need to slow down and drink less . . . ," he begged.

My heart seemed to stop. My emotions seemed dead. The tears and pain and aching couldn't have hurt any more than if I had literally been knifed or kicked. But the power of those emotions was not strong enough to make me renounce or forget the newfound love from God that I had experienced. I never wanted to return to that life of unrelieved guilt. Danny's words could not convince me to give up the respect that I had for myself and had begun to hold tightly to since making these new lifestyle decisions and keeping them.

There was a deafening silence in that mutually recognized moment of impasse.

Within days I made plans to leave California. We both knew it would be the best for us, as we still had intense feelings of love and passion for one another. But he was not ready, willing, or able to marry me, and I could not marry him if he had no desire to know or love God in the way that I did.

Our last conversation occurred in a rowboat on a moonlit lake, late into the evening one year later: a moment that might have been orchestrated for a proposal of marriage. There were no sounds, other than the oars softly splashing on the water. We drifted to the middle of the lake on that dark, hot summer night, and Danny said, "Becky, I'll never be the man you want me to be."

I had tried to lead him to God, and he would have none of it. The barrier between us became permanent.

I never expected to lose the first love in my life over the issue of sex. I was confused. Didn't sex equal love? Had I really been so foolish as to believe in that idea? To believe in the sexual license praised in the movies, sung about in romantic ballads on the radio, and discussed through the years with my friends in our "girl talk"? Unfortunately, yes, I had been foolish.

Through the loss of my relationship with Danny, I gained my self-respect—and a few insights about marriage, men, and sex. Whether I had been a sex object, a sex slave, or just plain stupid, I *finally* learned that sex didn't equal love, and that it was *love* that this young woman was looking for in a relationship.

Yet even after leaving a promiscuous lifestyle and becoming a Christian, I still remained confused about sexuality. How was it possible to experience healthy sexuality?

Eventually, I became engaged to a great Christian man, and we refrained from any sexual intimacy before our marriage. As our passions heated up before the honeymoon, my impressions of Christian sexuality came from my (mostly single) friends. At my wedding shower, for example, I was given warm, flannel nightgowns and a book called, *The Honeymoon Is Over*. I wondered if I should be more reserved in my sexual desires, . . . yet I assumed our marriage would be sexually satisfying to both of us.

But to my surprise, on my honeymoon, my strongest feelings were that it was my duty to satisfy Roger sexually. I began to think that biblical sex was a chore. I felt trapped, ashamed, and afraid to tell anyone how I felt. I was much too embarrassed to tell my husband how I felt, and proceeded to stifle my resentments and attempt to satisfy his sexual needs. I never seemed to have any desire for sex. Eventually, the sexual intimacy in my relationship with my husband began to suffer. We needed help. I needed help.

Going on a Sexual Healing Journey

Over the past sixteen years, my inhibitions, fears, resentments, and mental blocks have affected my marriage. I have gone through repeated cycles of avoiding sexual relations, growing guilty about withholding sexual intimacy, then admitting my inadequacies and inhibitions and asking for help. Because my husband's background is in counseling, we dealt with each step of my sexual healing journey through prayer, patience, confession, and counseling.

One of the oddest dilemmas has come from being able to enjoy sex physically, without ever getting past the many and various mental blocks or negative memories that plagued me. I often wondered if it would be possible for me to have a truly healthy sexual relationship.

I frequently speak in public about my past, and after one of my presentations, a couple felt compelled to come up and talk to me. They said, "Have you ever heard of 'The Seven Steps to Forgiveness Prayer' that Neil Anderson suggests for victims of sexual abuse?"

"Actually, I have heard of that prayer and have many friends who have prayed it," I answered, a bit reservedly, curious about where this conversation was leading.

"We would suggest that you get with a pastoral counselor and a woman friend who will join you in this prayer. It will take three hours to pray . . . ," they continued, assuming I would consider their idea.

I looked discerningly at this couple. Just that past weekend I had attended a Sexual Healing Retreat with my husband and about twenty other couples. My admissions and divulgences during our group sessions were by far my most detailed, troubled, and scarred. Even the leader met with my husband and me to encourage me to continue to pursue healing in this area. Although this couple's remarks about the seven-step prayer seemed unusual, their timing was uncanny, and it made me feel hopeful.

The minute I stepped off the airplane from my speaking engagement, I told my husband of this encounter. He called a counselor for me who prayed this seven-step prayer with people, and I called a woman friend to ask if she would join me for a special appointment to pray on the following Thursday.

As we sat in the counselor's office, I noticed the first thing that he did was to set the timer on his desk clock. It was 12:00 noon. Through each step of the prayer I confessed, admitted, remembered, and exposed all that I could about my sexual past. I even discovered certain correlations between my mental blocks and the frequent nightmares I had experienced over the past eighteen years. At the final "Amen," I heard the desk clock chime three times. Our counseling session had taken exactly three hours, just as the couple had mentioned.

No other chimes or bells went off. Though there was a matter-of-fact sense that a battle had been waged against the power of my past over my present, I felt that time itself would reveal the results of that prayer.

Over the next few months, my attitudes and actions were noticeably freer, but nightmares still harassed me enough to wake me up; I always found myself being chased or hunted down.

Then my last nightmare occurred. There was a person chasing me, and for the last time, he caught me. I almost recognized his face. I awoke, sitting straight up in bed. I then awoke my husband. Our conversation lasted an hour. I racked my brain to understand who the person was in my dream. Over the next few days, I couldn't put all the pieces together, but I could understand the significance of being abused—as I had been a number times by men before I was nineteen years old. I also realized that the abuse would never happen again. I came to the conclusion that those memories no longer could hurt me or have power over me!

The result of these experiences has been a sense of relief, peace, acceptance, strength, and even willing submission. There is definitely a renewed desire to love my spouse intimately as a gift *freely* given by me and to be mutually enjoyed by us. This certainly didn't happen overnight. But as I have begun to pursue my sexual healing aggressively, I have come closer and closer to finding and enjoying a truly healthy sexuality.*

For these reasons, I am compelled to tell my story, especially if it spares another woman from impulsive, compulsive, destructive sexual behavior. In recognizing my own ignorant thinking as a young woman, based on the misconception that sex equaled love, I often wished someone—whom I admired and respected—would have spoken to me of the privilege a woman has in maintaining her purity and virginity. I wish someone would have told me of the immeasurable respect a woman has for herself when she stands for what she believes. Had I been so taught, I believe I would have been a much different young woman.

Talking about Sex

From all that I've divulged about my sexual past, you can imagine that my personal approach to talking with young women about their sexuality certainly has not evolved from, "Do like I did." I share the difficult details of my own story and I end with, "*Don't* do what I did. It hurts. It leaves lasting scars. And the consequences that come with promiscuity often lead to shame and embarrassment that are not worth that lifestyle."

---

*If you think this type of prayer could be helpful to your situation, I would suggest that you contact Freedom in Christ Ministries at (310) 691-9128 for more information on Neil Anderson's books and prayers.

When I think back to the sexual attitudes of the 1960s and early 70s, I really can't think of *anyone* I knew in high school that didn't consider pregnancy as a possible result of intercourse! In fact, most of us were paranoid that sexual acts *less* extreme than intercourse might end up in pregnancy! (That misunderstanding probably kept us abstaining for a long time.) Therefore, when I hear the discussions and debates about condom distribution and the need for more intense sex education, I'm convinced that the difference between then and now is *not* the lack of information on *how* one gets pregnant, but the lack of *education* about the responsibilities *for* one's actions *after* one gets pregnant!

When abortion—the quick fix—wasn't an option, promiscuity just wasn't as popular. And when abstinence was considered the route for "good girls," sex before marriage was labeled as loose, even "slutty." But as the movies and music of our times showed and told us differently, one by one, we experimented.

After having lived in both worlds, I would like to think that the voices in our country that herald sexual morality should be given *at least* as much public respect as the other voices that advocate other sexual options; the voices of morality should also be given the courtesy and privilege of being promoted as credible. Abstinence as an option *deserves* to be heard and respected by the media.

Women of all ages and races are asking that a moral voice be heard—and applauded—in America. It seems time, and we hope it's not too late, for young women and men to be informed that, although it may be difficult, disciplines such as abstinence build character and self-esteem and integrity.

Instead of criticizing morality and abstinence, we should promote them. Why not encourage young men and women to take the steps necessary to be a "cut above," to stand tall for something, or to believe in themselves, or encourage them to live by standards that encourage reaching for a higher level of excellence?

I am only one of thousands pointing out to young women that just because "everyone is doing it" doesn't make it right. It doesn't mean he'll marry you, be faithful to you, or even that he loves you!

Where Can We Go from Here?

Because I am one of the sexually wounded women of America's past and present, I feel responsible to help young women avoid the sex-addiction or sex-abuse traps and the lies of free sex. If adults would affirm and teach young women and men how to have a healthy, non-promiscuous sexuality before their teenage years (by going out on dates with another couple or within a group of friends, by going out on dates *with* one's own family, and by maintaining certain boundaries with your date, such as not being in a house or bedroom alone), the number of unwanted pregnancies in America would decrease by the thousands, maybe even tens of thousands.

I believe that teaching abstinence as a viable, respectable, manageable option for young men and women is absolutely necessary in America today. To be effective, these ideas need to be taught with sincerity and conviction.

Most importantly, we cannot be afraid to teach young people that the basis for this teaching is from the Bible or to encourage them that God designed sex to be enjoyed *inside* the commitment of a marriage. We *can* remind young people, especially as they look around and see how sexually dysfunctional our nation has become, that promiscuity reaps many difficult, life-altering consequences, but that biblical sexuality promises security, health, and self-esteem. And we *can* honestly assure them that it is the only one hundred percent safe sex available—emotionally, spiritually, and physically. This form of sex education can best be taught in our homes by both fathers and mothers.

What Do You Expect?

Perhaps it's time for us to stop expecting so little of today's younger Americans by insisting that abstinence is unachievable! Young women and men *need* to be encouraged to respect themselves, to think highly of their treasure of sexuality. They need to be told much more than "It is impossible to wait for sex until you are married," or "You need to experiment sexually to be sure you are compatible," or that "Marriage is just an out-dated institution!"

Ah . . . but, they'll need role models. Maybe that's what we're afraid of. If we, as mature adults, can't understand sexuality and morality and fidelity, then how can we expect young people to abstain, to be morally pure, to remain faithful in marriage, or to respect members of the opposite sex as people, not objects?

It's time for those athletes, students, doctors, lawyers, teachers, laborers, entertainers, and politicians who *will* and *do* stand for sexual morality to speak out and be heard. And it is time for those who feel strongly about abstinence until marriage to look unashamedly for people of the opposite sex who will require the same!

It is time in our country to inspire young men and women to make a treasure of themselves; to think of themselves as a gift that they can give freely to the one who has *waited* just as long to make a lifelong commitment physically, emotionally, and sexually to them! To be God's wild and wonderful people, we need to be wildly devoted to our ideals.

But who will show young people the way? Models are hard to come by. Fortunately, I've had a number of wonderful people in my life, and I'd like to introduce you to a few of them and share the difference they made in my life.

Chapter Three

Make Me a Mentor

My First Mentor

I met Mrs. Carros when I was nineteen. She interviewed me for a job as the receptionist of a car dealership, where she was the business manager, an unusually high position for a woman in the auto industry at the time. She was in her late forties, perfectly manicured, and fashionably dressed every day. She was completely professional and highly refined in her manners, outer appearance, and business dealings.

In the interview, I gave her the impression that I was clean cut, pleasant, and professional. Perhaps she swallowed my act or observed some raw potential, but the bottom line was that she hired me! The entire first year that I worked for her, I pretended that I was a responsible person—until I could no longer cover up my vices.

I smoked two packs of cigarettes a day. She disliked this habit in professional women, but instead of asking or forcing me to quit, she gave me an incentive to stop. (I even got to choose my own reward—to drive her red custom convertible!) Her idea of rewarding me if I would quit smoking worked! After smoking for six years, the goal of getting to drive her car for a month was enough motivation to get me to stop a long-time habit!

Mrs. Carros didn't approve of my choice of boyfriends either. They would pick me up after work in noisy trucks and with outwardly displays of affection toward me on company grounds. But rather than giving darting looks of disapproval, she had little talks with me about respecting myself and "maintaining the appearance of a lady" while at the office.

My greatest cause of disappointment to Mrs. Carros must have been when I got into a head-on collision with my newly purchased car—a Chevrolet coupe I had purchased from our dealership. I had been driving under the influence of alcohol. Mrs. Carros never scolded or berated me. Instead, my boss and mentor displayed a measure of tolerance and counsel that went beyond any reprieve I had ever before experienced with an authority figure.

Through every crisis, mistake, problem, and dilemma, her office door always remained opened to me. I turned to her for advice more than any employee really had a right. Yet she would *always* listen, and then offer gentle but firm words of wisdom that came from years of experience. I had a tremendous respect for her. (Looking back, I believe this was the most compelling part of her character—she was respect-worthy.)

While working for her, my insatiable and uncontrollable appetite for alcohol and drugs overwhelmed me. Even though Mrs. Carros was my boss, she was one of the first people in whom I confided my alcoholism. Ironically, I was not afraid that she would fire me. Instead, I felt I had to reveal honestly the depth of my problem to her, believing that she would help me, that she even *loved* me. Though undeserving of her love, I felt confident—because of the kind of woman she had always been to me—that she would support me in my time of greatest need.

I was very fortunate to have Mrs. Carros as my boss, mentor, and friend when I was such an impressionable and confused young woman. No one expected more of me than she did, and no other woman had opened up to me greater business opportunities to stretch and better myself. As a mentor, she believed in me when no one else did—including myself. Through my substance abuse, boyfriends, car wrecks, and emotional scenes, she stood by me. Even upon my conversion to Christ, an unfamiliar occurrence to her, she continued to accept me and believe in me.

After becoming a Christian, I left California—and the auto industry—to return to my home in Cleveland. Later I went back to tell Mrs. Carros what an incredible impact she had upon my life, and though she had so many things "together" and was such a wonderful teacher, I still wanted to share the spiritual dimension of my life with her. She had seen how dramatically God had changed me, but I wanted her to share in my inner peace and joy.

I would write to her and occasionally visit, always sharing with her about my personal relationship with God. Eventually, after five years, she wrote back to me; she too had recently asked Christ into her life and now fully understood the conversion experience I had had while working for her!

Sadly, the Mrs. Carroses—those strong, unselfish, powerful mentoring women—have been rare jewels in my life.

From Hitting Bottom to Hitting the Glass Ceiling

Shortly after leaving California and the car dealership, and upon returning home, I embarked on a career that I had never dreamed of pursuing. As a result of struggling with alcohol and drugs, and then finding God, I stumbled into the field of youth work. Walking into the office of my former high school principal, I shared the story of my new Christian lifestyle and my desire to tell high school kids about having a personal relationship with God! He thought I had "gone overboard," and reminded me that my nice story was religious and therefore inappropriate for a *public* school! Convinced that I had the answers to the problems and questions kids have about family, sex, and life after death, I continued to search for a place where my message might fit.

A few months later, I went to work for a Christian youth organization, first as a volunteer, then as an intern, and finally as a paid employee. Initially I was content to answer the phones, collect camp money, and organize programs simply because this secretarial work was what women normally did. I never spent time thinking about the differing roles between men and women in Christian work; it was just an unspoken rule in the seventies that women were organizers and secretaries, so they were not encouraged to lead Ciub meetings, give "talks," or supervise other staff.

As I continued to help with the administration and organization, other more natural gifts began to flow from me: leadership, teaching, and speaking. Because our organization was small enough, there were more opportunities to lead and teach than we had leaders or teachers—male or female! Therefore, I was regularly delegated assignments that fit my personality profile and utilized my people and communication skills.

Men as Mentors

While on my journey over the past eighteen years, I have sought women who would lead, encourage, build, believe in, and mentor me; women who would open up doors of opportunity so that I could make a mark—a difference—in my world. But despite Mrs. Carros' influence, my experience has been that many of those mentoring women role models either aren't out there, don't have power, or are too busy fending for themselves. Though not all women find this to be the case, for the most part, I have looked to men to train, advise, help, and mentor me.

Although not all the men I have known or worked with have been eager to build up, teach, encourage, share, and empower women, some have been exceptionally open to seeing women realize their potential and use their gifts.

My first and favorite male mentor (at that time and even to this day) was my boss, who eventually became my best friend and husband, Roger. His style of training and delegation was the exception rather than the rule, since he didn't divide his work force into "the men do this" and "the women do that" categories, but assessed our strengths and delegated the work accordingly. What was the bottom line? We had more kids who needed leaders than we had leaders to go around—men or women! So we all worked overtime to meet the needs of the many kids we worked with in Cleveland. I did anything and everything that I could dream of or had a desire to do—on the local level.

Still, women often find they can only rise to a certain point. But if you are going to hit a "glass ceiling" in social work or Christian youth work, it usually happens at the regional and national levels. When I really began to improve and develop in my skills and experiences as a youth worker and communicator this discouraging reality became clear. Although I was as active in my ministry, as successful a club director, and possibly even as gifted a communicator as any of the men who held similar positions, I was never asked to present a workshop at an event outside of the Cleveland area. Event after event, workshop after workshop, convention after convention, I observed that those who were invited to communicate to peers or students in the Christian arena were—and still are—ninety-five to ninety-nine percent of the time men! Although fifty percent or more of most youth or adult Christian audiences are women, men are the speakers.

Every denomination has its own theological position on the subject of a woman's role in the church, of course, and in recent years, many denominations' doctrinal positions regarding the profile and place of women in ministry has become more negotiable. The more dogmatic a church or organization is about this issue, the fewer opportunities women have to teach and lead. My personal conviction is that the individuals most injured by these disputes and closed doors are young women.

Especially in youth work, the traditional, rigid, theological positions about women not being allowed or encouraged to speak or teach are absolutely backfiring. By hindering strong, young Christian women leaders and communicators from being role models in forums from small youth group meetings to large youth events, rigid traditionalism defeats the same conservative values of wholesomeness and faithfulness in the family and the church that it treasures.

Simply, if young women have no public role models other than funky music divas or twenty-year-old actresses, then those of us encouraging morality and excellence in young women should not be surprised with some of the choices these students are making!

Young women are absolutely *looking* for, longing for, and hungry to see and emulate exciting, powerful women. I feel strongly that it should be a top priority of the church to be enthusiastically raising up godly, strong, skilled women as speakers, teachers, and leaders for young men and women alike.

Because I was brought up in a mainline Protestant denomination and have worked mostly with and for parachurch organizations, I have been very comfortable in accepting nontraditional leadership positions for women. As a young Christian woman with an exciting, life-changing story, I saw my role as a woman communicator to be like that of a high school teacher or coach. I personally did not think of myself as a minister, although I found pastoral skills necessary in caring for a group of students.

In addition, working for a parachurch youth organization, rather than for a church, better fit my personality and skills as there was simply more freedom and a less restrictive structure. (In general, I find a church is more comfortable with men in leadership roles and women carrying the assisting, secretarial positions.)

When I look back, I still wonder who were the potential women mentors for those of us who were young women communicators. At that time, my role models were the *men* who wrote, spoke, and communicated to youth on a national level. By the mid eighties, there were very few, if any, young women *regularly* on national or even regional youth platforms or in positions of national leadership, much less financially and logistically able to mentor—or train up—younger women communicators and leaders.

It wasn't until 1986 that I found myself in the right place at the right time. Wanting very much to have the opportunity to tell my story (of overcoming alcohol with God's help) to more American students, I attended a National Youth Worker's Convention where—at last—I could network! (Just for the record, none of the platform speakers at that particular convention were women, but a handful of women taught workshops. The field of Christian youth work, in which I have lived and worked for many years, *is* a man's world.)

At that convention, I literally bumped into Mike Yaconelli, the founder of a youth organization called Youth Specialties. To make amends for almost running me down, he took a moment to ask me what I did. I blurted out that I was an author and speaker. He asked for my card and mentioned that his traveling youth speaker's team, Grow for It, was actively looking to hire a woman communicator! (I remembered thinking, "Only in progressive California!") Two months later, I found myself in San Diego training with a team of eight other youth speakers, all men!

Again, I was resigned to the fact that my mentors would be men. But our common ground was that each of us had a passion for reaching kids in America with the Good News that God loves them and has a plan for their lives. Isn't that what Christian youth work is really all about?

Over the next three years I struggled with my self-image, my identity, and my communication style as it compared to the men on my team. I couldn't believe how timid I became in a brainstorming meeting with eight unknown men. Normally, I am pretty fun, sometimes funny, fairly confident, and always opinionated. It took me over a year to discern which moments of silence were born out of my own female insecurity or a result of being purposely antagonized or intimidated. Unfortunately, during those three years, I endured more hours of inner scrutiny than I enjoyed out doing my job.

In this setting I began to understand the differing speaking styles of men and women. Over time I found that my speaking style as a woman contained more "feeling and emotion," which came from real-life stories, with all their humor. My male counterparts more effectively and easily delivered scripted talks, told lots of great, humorous anecdotes, and could pull off planned jokes. My attempts at the same presentations fell flat.

The process of finding my place and purpose as a woman communicator on a team of mostly men was grueling! I spent hours crying, but only when no one could see me. I even lost weight from the pressure of being constantly evaluated on my performance and personality. After reading some of my peers' evaluations, I realized that not all men respected or appreciated women communicators.

I often felt my peers were confused by my conservative views in not using profanity and by my conviction that, if you are a youth worker, you should abstain from alcohol. Even my commitment to an hour of daily prayer seemed to make my peers uncomfortable. I wasn't sure if they thought I was trying to be "holier than thou" or just a fussy woman. In truth, I leaned toward a more conservative lifestyle as a result of the devastating effect alcohol had in my life, as well as the influence of the ten years I spent as a youth worker in the more conservative Midwest.

The men seemed equally unsure of how to deal with me. Some treated me as "one of the guys," while others acted distant. There were times that I would feel left out when my traveling partners would pair up together on the plane, and I would be left to sit alone. A few of the guys treated me more like they treated their wives: They would open doors for me and help carry my luggage because *they* were more comfortable relating to me that way. Everyone did strive to maintain strictly platonic friendships throughout each season of travel and long hours of development meetings. After one year, another woman joined the team!

After three years of little personal success or satisfaction, I forged out on my own as a speaker. The mounting loneliness and stigma attached to being one of only two women on a team full of men, as well as the recognition that I had a heart for evangelism and prayer, rather than scripted talks we would all give in separate locations, made my departure inevitable. But what started out as a frustration turned into an acknowledgment and growing confidence that I, as a woman, had my own unique message to share with American students and adults—and a motivational style of my own. The deepest call in my heart that I could identify was that I was created and called to be a communicator.

Mentors Inspire Mentors

A leader is always looking for someone to challenge them to grow, offer them wise counsel, share a bit of practical advice, and even give them a word of hope. I *have* been fortunate in the last ten years to find a woman who inspired me and hundreds of other women in those ways. Florence Littauer is a motivational author and speaker and the founder of Christian Leaders And Speakers Seminar (CLASS). Florence mentored not only me, but hundreds of women who aspire to write and speak professionally.

Although she travels extensively throughout the world as a motivational speaker and author, Florence also holds a number of speaker training workshops several times each year in various regions of the United States and Canada. What motivates her? If the truth be known, these workshops are probably the most financially and physically draining of all of the events she holds. But Florence continues to train women—and men—of all ages in the art of presenting *their* story. She believes that well-trained communicators will more effectively share their life-changing stories and be able to say it with CLASS!

Because Florence has modeled that a woman who is *able* to train and encourage other women should do so, I've been encouraged to take a step toward helping younger women communicators. In 1993, I enlisted the help of two young women, Kara Eckman of San Diego and Diane Elliot, the founder of a women's youth worker journal called *Journey*. Together we hosted the First Annual Women In Youth Ministry Conference in April of 1994 in the Chicago area with sixty-five women in attendance!

The results were phenomenal! Women were trained to speak, encouraged to pursue their call in various youth ministry positions, sincerely challenged to use their gifts to make a difference, and charged to broaden their horizons! More than anything else, I wanted to encourage each of them that there were many opportunities available to women who have been called and empowered *by God* to love and nurture kids back to him. In April of 1995, *Journey* magazine will host the Second Annual Women In Youth Ministry Conference, and I will continue in the coming years to train young women to be WISE: Women Impacting and Setting Examples for younger women—through one-day workshops! (Thank you for your inspiration, Florence!)

Books and Their Authors Are Our Mentors

On many occasions I have been inspired and motivated to believe that my life *could and would* change while hearing an inspirational speaker speak, but it can also happen while reading a motivational book. My fondest memory of a person who unknowingly mentored me occurred a decade ago, in February 1984.

Along with three hundred other women, I attended a workshop on prayer by Karen Mains, an author and radio personality. That workshop was the catalyst to prompt me to make prayer a priority in my life. At the close of her one-hour presentation on prayer, I was moved to make a radical decision to pray for one hour a day for the rest of my life! Not only have I kept the commitment that I made at the end of her workshop over ten years ago, but something else just as outrageous occurred.

Shortly after the workshop I boarded the down escalator at the hotel. Karen Mains was on the other side, heading up. Startled, excited, and fueled by my brand new passion for prayer, I looked her right in the eye and said quickly, "Karen, I really believe God used you to speak to me. Someday I am going to write a book about prayer!" She just smiled, but I felt accountable to my words.

Really, what are the odds that I could ever fulfill that assertion? By November 1984, I had written and self-published *My Partner Prayer Notebook*. Today, this work has sold over 100,000 copies, and in addition, I have written a book to teach people to journal their prayers, *Let Prayer Change Your Life*, and a book sharing my excitement about prayer in *Wild Things Happen When I Pray!*

I love that story. It convinces me that I don't have to know or even meet my mentors to be powerfully influenced by them! (You'll find a list of my "books as mentors" at the end of this chapter.)

Be a Mentor

Though few women have a job description like mine, some important and wonderful women friends in my life keep me accountable for maintaining a balanced family life, stretch me to reach toward dreams and goals, love to laugh with me, choose to work out with me, and encourage me to dream. They are also quick to remind me that even if we don't have women in our lives to mentor us, we can *be* mentors!

Every one of us who cares about the future of this nation can—and should—become a mentor by simply becoming a small group leader or a volunteer in an organization that leads, influences, and cares for young people. Organizations such as the Girl Scouts or Boy Scouts, church youth groups, 4H, Big Brothers and Big Sisters are *begging* for volunteer leaders who will become "significant others" in the lives of the many directionless, sometimes parentless kids in America. In addition, most junior and senior high schools hire qualified adults from their community to be coaches and aides, opening wide the doors for concerned adults to help.

And even though we might find the pay is small to none, the reward for the time given and the influences made by *any* significant adult in the lives of young men and women will be the lasting impression left on them that someone, especially God, cares for them. We may not be able to share openly our personal convictions or beliefs in public schools or certain organizations, but being a caring, friendly adult in a young person's life often provides them not only a role model, but also immeasurable healing and hope.

Don't be surprised if the fulfillment you receive from helping or mentoring a young person becomes the greatest benefit of all.

But to be effective, you can't let your emotions get in the way. That's our next battle.

Books That Have Been Mentors to Me

The Bondage Breaker by Neil T. Anderson
Growing Up Addicted by Steve Arterburn
Pursuit of Holiness by Jerry Bridges
Lord, Change Me by Evelyn Christenson
Loving God by Chuck Colson
Prayer by O. Hallesby
Personality Plus by Florence Littauer
Ordering Your Private World by George MacDonald

Beyond Ourselves by Catherine Marshall
A Man Called Peter by Catherine Marshall
Something More by Catherine Marshall
Love Hunger by Frank Minirth and Paul Meier
The Prayer Life by Andrew Murray
With Christ in the School of Prayer by Andrew Murray
Disciplines of a Beautiful Woman by Anne Ortlund
Why Revival Tarries by Leonard Ravenhill

Chapter Four

Mom's Bad Mood

It was that time of the month. I was having a bad day. My son, Jake, at the time a fifth-grader, was also having a bad day. He had misplaced his baseball mitt, and we were hurrying out the door to his Little League game. Exasperated, I said, "Look, take Daddy's mitt. But if you lose Daddy's mitt, you are going to get the biggest lickin' of your lifetime." He knew I was serious!

After he pitched a great game, we piled the gear and ourselves into the car and headed home. As we pulled in the driveway, I looked inquisitively at my son and asked, "Jakey, where's Daddy's baseball mitt?"

With sheer horror on his face, he put both of his little, stubby hands up to his cheeks and screeched, "Oh no, I left it at the field."

Two houses to the left and two houses to the right heard me scream at the top of my lungs, "Jacob Anthony Tirabassi." Then I stormed into the house—a lesson I am sure I had learned from my past—turned right around and stormed back out through the garage and into the car. Before the little gipper had a chance to say another word, we plowed backward out of the driveway and took off for the field.

Jake, having seen me pray in times of great need and desperation, thought it best to try this himself. He said aloud, "Dear Jesus, . . ."

I turned to him, pointed my finger at his nose and barked, "Don't even pray!" (Now *that* is out of control.)

As my son hopped out of the car and ran up to the coach, I could see that his Daddy's mitt had been picked up and saved to be returned to us. It didn't matter. I was still furious. I wanted to lay into my little son for his irresponsibility—and any other frustration that I could come up with that would make me feel better!

As we screeched out of the parking lot, back toward home for the second time, I realized that I had overreacted. Not wanting to fully admit this to my son, I said, "Jake, maybe it's just the wrong time of the month?" He said, "You mean that MBM?"

"What's that?" I asked.

He said, "Mom's bad mood."

"No, Jake," I continued, "it's called PMS."

He didn't stop there. He said, "Can little boys get that? . . . 'Cuz I've been getting in a lot of trouble and losing a lot of things lately."

"No, Jake, little boys can't get that."

After a formal apology, which he nonchalantly accepted, I thought the discussion would be over.

It was . . . until his fifth-grade teacher was having a bad day a few months later.

The classroom had been out of control after moving into a new building. His teacher, usually funny and lighthearted, raised her voice and began yelling at the class to "*Be Quiet!*" My son, concerned about her growing irritability, raised his hand.

When the teacher called on Jake, he simply asked, "Mrs. B., could this be the wrong time of the month?"

Well, to say the least, neither the teacher, nor the class (nor the other elementary teachers or even the principal who heard the story later in the teacher's lounge) were able to keep a straight face for the rest of the day!

In fact, when I showed up at the classroom door at 3:00 P.M., Mrs. B. was still crying from laughing so hard throughout the day. After she told me, through hysterical bouts of laughter, what my son had said, she remarked, "Becky, this is the best line in twenty years of teaching!" She added that when she had called home and told her husband what Jacob had said, all he could ask was, "How did he know?"

Women Are Predictably Unpredictable!

Women have intense feelings and desires, vacillating from anger to excitement in the same day and with the same people! We are insecure one moment and presumptuous the next. We are emotional. The range of our feelings varies like a seismograph recording tremblers in the Los Angeles area on any given day—unpredictable.

At times . . .

We feel insecure when we're filling the shoes of a man before us or are at a meeting where we are the only woman amidst all men.

We feel insecure when we're being patronized or put down.

We feel insecure when we find ourselves pretending, instead of just being confident in who we are.

We feel insecure when we know that the expectations upon us as women are greater than on men who do what we do!

We feel insecure and discouraged when other women make it difficult for us to succeed. (I know, it's a terrible thought.)

We feel insecure when we are perceived as threatening, rather than considered as strong women, inwardly motivated, outwardly assertive.

We feel insecure when people tell us what they've heard or assumed about us and it's not true. (Why didn't they just ask us first?)

We feel insecure when we are misunderstood for being intense rather than focused.

We feel insecure when we are hindered from having an impact on the world, simply because we *are* women.

When do we feel secure? When we confidently admit to ourselves that God has called us, that *he* believes in us, that *he* has a plan for our lives, and that he has given us skills and talents to make a difference in our world. We feel secure when we are in loving, committed relationships.

But insecurity is not our only emotional hurdle to overcome.

We feel afraid when . . .

. . . we are on the brink of success.

. . . we think someone looks at us and is angry that we have a better life.

. . . we think we are going to be rejected.

. . . friends get divorced and their lives and their children's lives are a mess.

. . . we are getting wrinkled and old-looking.

We feel angry . . .

. . . when the bank messes up.

. . . when we have to wait in line—any line!

. . . when we lose information that we have input on the computer.

. . . when we're ignored.

. . . when we're lied to.

. . . when we spill or splash something on our good suit or blouse.

. . . when we miss the sale price or the "last one" of something.

. . . when someone takes advantage of us.

We feel fat when . . .

. . . we see or meet someone who is in terrific shape.

. . . we have had too much to eat in one day or even in one meal.

. . . we try to find something to wear and can't squeeze into a pair of blue jeans that fit just great *before* they were washed and dried on high heat!

. . . we are noticeably bloated.

. . . someone asks us if we have lost weight, and in actuality, we have put on a few pounds! (bummer)

Some feelings are more individual. For myself . . .

I hate when I feel competitive or jealous.

And I feel jealous when someone is able to do something that I have not even had the audacity to try.

And I feel overly competitive *even* when I am winning at tennis *or* Scrabble!

I feel jealous when I am looking in at those who are looking out.

I feel competitive when I think I can do something better than someone who is doing it right now.

I feel jealous when I see someone who has not had to "pay their dues" yet has been handed the fast track to success. (Oh, well, that's life!)

Then there is the "hot" topic of politics. Truthfully, I feel politically confused . . . *a lot*. (Is there really such a thing as politically correct?)

Then there are those feelings of helplessness . . .

. . . when I see hungry or homeless people in the same places day after day.

. . . if a person doesn't return my phone call or ignores me.

. . . when I would visit my one hundred-year-old grandma who lived in a nursing home in a constant state of dementia.

. . . when a child is reported missing.

. . . when the road less traveled is the one I'm on.

. . . when I am misunderstood.

And along with so many women I have felt (notice the past tense) abused . . .

. . . when I lived with a guy who never asked me to marry him.

. . . in any number of situations where I was the only woman and was too intimidated to speak, share, or even joke around for fear of being rejected or misunderstood.

. . . when I allowed myself to "give in" to people who really didn't care about me, anyway.

. . . by parents who screamed and yelled and hollered, not understanding how vulnerable I was as a child or how much their actions were their own coping mechanisms for survival.

. . . by men who took advantage of me when I had too
   much to drink.

Then there is the feeling of powerlessness that comes over
me . . .

. . . when I feel myself being controlled by others.
. . . when I believe that my self-image is based on what
   others think about me, rather than what God thinks
   about me.
. . . when I think people want to hurt me.
. . . when I wallow in self-pity.
. . . when I tell myself "it" can't be done, temporarily for-
   getting that I really believe that "with God, all things
   are possible."

But feeling powerless is not *all* bad—it is also a great beginning place. When our lives are at the brink of being un-
manageable, we can acknowledge our need for God's help and
intervention. In our greatest weaknesses and failures, we can
receive hope, find answers, and ultimately be rescued by God!

In fact, it is my daily relationship with God that allows me
to meet the challenges I face. Because I am a child of God, I
feel capable . . .

. . . for any task I've signed up to do, *if* I've done my
   homework.
. . . of speaking in front of any size audience, because I
   believe that God, my Creator, has given me a life-
   changing message to share.
. . . of making a difference in my country for what is right
   and true and good. (Or at least I'm going to die trying!)
. . . of making friends with anyone I meet—rich or poor,
   famous or common, young or old.

. . . of being a good wife and mom, while at the same time following my dreams.

. . . of being a *relevant* Christian woman in this country!

. . . of living a balanced life.

When I am living a balanced life, I feel fit . . .

. . . when I have worked out either in a gym, with a video, or on my bike at least three times a week, preferably four.

. . . when my clothes from last year, same season, still fit—and comfortably!

. . . when I realize that a great-looking gal who just walked in the room is skinnier and prettier, but I'm not jealous, because I'm at a good place for me.

. . . when a friend of mine says, "Hey, you look great!" (Thanks!)

. . . when I've done sit-ups for at least a month!

And it is the influence of God in my life that causes me to feel committed . . .

. . . to my husband, until death do us part.

. . . to my extended family.

. . . to this country and it's founding principles of freedom, truth, and equality.

. . . to speaking and writing to teenagers, until I'm too old or they no longer listen to me!

. . . to being a woman of integrity.

. . . to God.

There is nothing that can replace my feeling of peace . . .

. . . when a Christian friend or family member dies, knowing they have gone to heaven and that I will see them there someday.

. . . when I hear God's voice in my heart.

. . . when I sit outside and talk to God.

And my very deepest feelings revolve around a sense of being called . . .

> . . . to be a relevant Christian in a country that no longer has a true picture of what a Christian stands for, looks like, and lives for!
>
> . . . to reach my generation with the life-changing Good News of Jesus' love.
>
> . . . to be a wild, wonderful woman for God.

All women have a unique assortment of emotions, feelings, memories, pain, and passions. These give us our faith, flavor, and beauty. They make us exactly who we are—and who we are meant to be! I contend that the women of my generation have struggled uniquely. We have wrangled and agonized over how to be good wives and moms within this country's current economic demands upon a family's income. We have been exhilarated and challenged educationally and vocationally as boundaries are being pushed back, offering us incredible opportunities previously unavailable to the generations of women before us. Yet with the onslaught of pornography in the marketplace and sexual harassment in the workplace, we have fought to be appropriately assertive, feminine, sexual, and friendly. And our generation has experienced the added pressure of having one's faith in God portrayed by the media as weakness, rather than as the source of one's strength and pride. We have grown up during a time when right can be labeled wrong, and wrong is often heralded as right.

We are women who find ourselves in need of relief from these stresses and many of us have found such help in nontraditional options.

Chapter Five

The Helpmate Needs Help

The Options Begin at the Beginning

We had been married only one year and ten days when we had our first son. When I married my husband, we both felt "called" to youth work and agreed that we worked best as a team. In fact, we enjoyed working side by side! Therefore, after our son was born, we made a decision not to have more than one child. We agreed that the greatest daytime responsibility for our son would be mine, so I resumed work only as a volunteer. This enabled me to have the freedom to work or stay at home depending on my son's schedule, health, and development.

This volunteer arrangement worked quite well for the first year, but once we got into a "groove" with naps and meals, and

61

after making it successfully through six months of the "insepa-rable" stage (called nursing), I started to grow restless.

Staying home with an infant was as difficult for me as fol-lowing a slow tractor on a country road in a no-passing zone. It was very hard for me to limit my activities with high school kids, as well as put my college education and earning potential on hold.

I can't say I was patient or stoic, content or settled during my "at-home-mom" stage of life, but I did remain at home for about one year, believing this best for my son.

At that juncture, because I needed and wanted to return to youth work, I found creative ways to return to my position on a part-time basis. By working out of my home a majority of the time, I managed to make my calls, plan meetings, and go into the office only once a week. I never considered public day care; I felt more comfortable rotating baby-sitting between an aunt who was at home on Tuesdays and a friend who was an "at-home" mom and had a child who was the same age as my son, Jacob. In addition, my mom and dad spent about ten hours a week, mostly evenings, playing with, singing to, and feeding healthy food to their grandson while I spent time working with high school kids, coaching cheerleaders, and planning meetings with the volunteers.

Being a part-time working mom was the perfect way for *me* to balance my commitments to my family values and still fulfill my desire to work with high school kids. And because we lived from paycheck to paycheck, the extra pay—though small—made our financial ends meet much more easily.

Enter the Guilt

Early in my marriage, well-meaning Christian women regularly encouraged me to have more children. But having more children was not Roger's or my personal desire. Instead of just admitting that my deepest desires were different than those of the Christian women around me, I constantly found myself living under a shadow of guilt for not wanting to have more children, and not wanting to give up my work with students in the local community.

The result? I often felt more embarrassed or ashamed than proud of my work with youth. I felt terrible about myself and angry at them when women who would say, "I'm praying for you to have another baby!" I'd cringe with fear that I might get pregnant! I expected one day to receive a letter of condemnation from the women who felt that a young mother should have a quiver full of children and not be working outside the home.

My confusion only grew as I observed many successful, dynamic women who had children *and* who either held paid positions outside of their homes (often in the church) or volunteered in non-profit organizations, spending many hours a week, mobilizing and encouraging others.

I continually struggled to find a personal balance between remaining true to traditional family values *and* the call I felt to respond to the needs of the many hurting kids and families in my community.

After much inner searching and praying to God about what God would have *me* to do, I finally found a comfort level where I could both work and be at home. I made decisions in which my son and husband did not feel a sense of compromise, and was flexible enough to change with the seasons of my life *and* in my son's growth and development. I began to carve out for myself a non-traditional, but value-driven role as a contemporary Christian woman.

By the time Jake entered pre-school, I would run to the office two or three days a week and be back in time to pick him up. As kindergarten started, I would fill the free hours in each half day with writing, planning, contacting, and spending quiet devotional time either at home or at the office. By one o'clock, after lunch and errands, Jake would nap, then at 3:00 P.M. we would go to the high school for cheerleading practice. That little guy ran through the high school halls, introducing me to key football and basketball players, and even was potty-trained in the high school restrooms!

Eventually, as my responsibilities grew as a leader with the young women staff and students, having a little boy meant that at campouts and retreats, Jake would have to stay with his dad and "the boys," rather than with mom.

When Jake was old enough to stay up late, he loved to go to youth group and athletic events. And though he was a boisterous, ball-throwing, wrestle-with-the-guys kind of boy, he somehow understood the line between being quiet during an hour long meeting and being in the "middle of the pile" before and after the meeting! At last report, Jake (now fifteen) has mentioned that he might like to be a junior high youth worker! (I guess he hasn't seen another profession in which you can rollerblade, ski, surf, have great relationships—and get paid for it!)

A Road Well Traveled

I now realize that my journey to be and feel like a good mom as well as a productive, dynamic part of society in these last fifteen years has followed a well traveled road.

In America, many women who are moms work.

Some have to support and raise their children by themselves, most often due to divorce. Others hold part-time positions to make the extra money to send their kids to college. Still other women have an equal or higher income than their husbands. The more employable spouse at a given time might be the wife.

Because working women are meeting and marrying working men, sacrifice and change for *both* spouses is inevitable. To tell a woman that she should not work, but must stay at home to be the conventional, traditional woman of the past, does not address the way people live today. To suggest options, such as part-time work, an at-home office, or entrepreneurism as viable options for women is to face reality in America and to offer practical help.

The Practical "How-To's"

In each of my work situations over the past fifteen years, I have had to negotiate aggressively my office hours, vacations, raises, and work station. For example, by asking for more time off, rather than regular raises, I was able to spend the summer months at home with my son during his elementary school years. And now, because I am self-employed, I schedule very few speaking engagements during the summer for the very same reason.

Because I've had a child most of my married life, I have always opted to work part-time (which brought with it less money and benefits than a full-time position) to assure that I would be home at 3:00 P.M. (when school let out), rather than working until 5:00 P.M., the "normal" work day. By making the choices that were right for me and my family on a daily—and seasonal—basis, we were always able to avoid child-care or day-care situations and their expenses. Of course, sometimes day-care is unavoidable for women whose other options are limited. Still, it can be part of an overall creative solution to balancing work and home life.

But these choices brought other consequences; we have never had much of a savings account, retirement account, or driven new cars. (In fact, we never even bought our own color television until 1988 and our first new refrigerator came home in 1994.) But these material concessions allowed me to better handle *my* family responsibilities, while still making a significant impact in my community—and now country—within the framework that best suited my family's lifestyle.

To make this work, I had to brainstorm, search out, consider, look for, try, and simply *ask* my employer what options were available or negotiable. In each situation, we had to make choices such as living on less income, accepting non-traditional roles (especially for my husband), putting an office in our home, and creatively working out part-time and evening-hour schedules. Through these flexible options I was able to find the balance that both my husband and I were comfortable with so that we could maintain our family values, while still allowing me to pursue my personal dreams. (During one "season," I even sold Tupperware in order to buy my first electric typewriter!)

Every working mom needs to make choices that do not take a toll on her child or children, weighing sacrifices of time, money, and expenditure of energy, knowing that these sacrifices will reap immeasurably satisfying rewards *over time*. Looking back, I believe my strongest asset was a personal conviction to weigh my "to do" list and my "dream" list *in light of my responsibilities as a wife and mom!*

The Career Woman

The growing trend among women from all walks of life in America is to stay home with their young children, opting to put their careers on hold to be their children's major caretakers.

Magazine articles are full of women from the corporate, entertainment, and education sectors who are staying at home to raise their families. Upon deciding to have children, women are reducing their work hours and travel and increasing their at-home time. In addition, many women are choosing to divide parenting with their husbands.

The greatest challenge for the career woman is to stay current and focused in her field during her child-bearing and parenting years. (The man who shares deeply in parental duties faces the same challenge.) And though it may cost her a career "rung," by being willing to stay involved in her profession—even if at a distance (through classes, reading, or volunteer membership)—she has the option either to resume where she left off when she is ready and able or even to "take off" in a new direction!

Women are finding that the very tension between their dreams and their values will cause them to schedule their daily lives more realistically and creatively, be more willing to wait, and yet never give up the pursuit of their personal goals and dreams! As women, we are most successful and effective as moms and wives when we continually align and adjust our priorities to fit each stage of our lives.

The Nineties Woman

Can the nineties woman raise a healthy, happy family and pursue a career in this economy? Not without help!

In 1989, after working with and for my husband for over ten years, we believed it was the "scheduled" time in my life for me to pursue my dreams of writing and speaking. I was growing restless of working in one location and was ready to step out into a new adventure for my life work.

But when the realities of having a traveling wife finally hit Roger, he was reluctant to let me move forward. His questions were valid: Who would take care of Jacob when I traveled? How would we replace my income? What made me think there was a need or market for what I wanted to do?

By playing the "devil's advocate," my husband made me fine tune my dreams into realistic, achievable goals. By developing a workshop series, taking speaker's training classes, establishing a fee system that would both cover the expenses of an office and equal that of the income I would be giving up, and tapping into my various networks, I was at last able to convince my husband—who was also my boss—that he should let me forge out on this new trail.

Within the first six months, the pieces quickly began to fall together. The calls to book speaking engagements started to come in, and my first two books actually began to sell copies! But soon the demand on me, both professionally and on the home front, became greater than I could handle alone.

My boss/mentor/friend/husband made a "head of the house" decision: "Becky, if your work is growing in demand and you want to pursue this, then because our son is only in junior high school—a very critical time of development for a young boy—I feel I need to leave the demands of the full-time director position and look for some type of part-time work that will allow me to be available at 3:00 P.M. (when school lets out) and to be free on the weekends when you travel." I was surprised—not by his assessment of the situation, but by his willingness to look for a non-traditional solution.

My husband, Roger, is eight years older than I am. He has a doctor of ministry degree, a master's in guidance and counseling, as well as a master of divinity. After working five years in a public school system, he spent the next ten years as the executive director of Greater Cleveland Youth for Christ. He then became the director of youth ministry at a large Southern California church for five more years. Having worked with high school students for over twenty years, his deepest desire, especially after dealing with and counseling so many troubled students and families, was to raise our son in the most secure and healthy family situation possible. He also knew that I had waited for over ten years, since we first had met and married, to follow my dream of writing and speaking. If *now* was the time for me to step out, now should be the time for him to take a non-traditional role by being more of an at-home parent.

The Blessings and Benefits of Non-Traditional Roles

Roger's sacrifice has had repercussions that are still being felt in our family to this day. First, having worked so hard with kids over twenty years, he never was able to slow down enough to develop the crisis-counseling materials he had written for his dissertation. Now he can.

The plan to pursue a part-time job allowed him to work with an organization that was willing and ready to incorporate Roger's materials into a Twelve Step Program with their teenagers. After an interim year of part-time work, training youth workers for another local Christian organization, my husband was employed (again part-time) to write materials, create a format, train volunteers, and design a unique model of a Twelve Step Program for hurting kids, called Lifelines. This position actually provided him the freedom to be at home after school and on weekends, as well as time necessary to create, write, and develop his own program. In addition, Lifelines has significantly helped the families in our community.

Another benefit of my husband's new role has been that our son, Jacob, now a high school student, has had the opportunity to spend extended weekend hours with his father—

motorcycling, remote-control car racing, playing Super-nintendo, golfing, attending sporting events, and going to trading-card shows. The weekly hours that my son and husband spend together put to shame the national statistics about dads who spend only ten quality minutes a day with their children.

For me, the blend of an at-home office, a weekend travel schedule, and a full-time assistant, has put me at home more hours in a week than when I worked in an office and held a part-time local job!

For those who are skeptical or even cynical, I would assure you that the benefits of having and developing non-traditional roles for our family has not been a blow to my husband's ego, but instead has allowed him to work for thirty hours doing what he loves, instead of working fifty plus hours putting out urgent fires and always trying to catch up with a heavy work-load of counseling, administrating, and fund-raising. It has pro-vided the time for a great relationship to develop between a high school son and his dad, which so very few young boys have an opportunity to do these days. And it has allowed me, a wife and mom, to explore alternative solutions for bringing in-come into our family budget without going into an office. (I even sold Tupperware—twice!)

I feel very fortunate that I have equally shared my child's upbringing with his father. Not that we keep a record of the hours or seasons when one of us has spent more time than the other nurturing, disciplining, doing homework with, playing, or teaching our son, but daily we both work at loving our child. We knew from the start that for both of us to work *and* to have children would mean a conscious effort to maintain balance in our marriage and work responsibilities. We simply have re-mained committed to our values, to each other, to our child, and to God.

Ideal Versus Realistic

I believe that the heart's desire of most women is to raise their own little ones. But very often in America today, that is simply not possible.

It's also important to stress that the many moms who do not have to work or *choose* not to work, and are able to live on their husband's income or on a lower income, *in order to stay at home with their children*, have made an equally noble choice. Together these couples have determined that the husband will handle all of the financial liabilities.

Counting the Cost

Before children enter into the family dynamics, each woman—you—have a variety of decisions to face:

Are you willing to sacrifice your career when you have children?

Will you personally raise your children until they attend school?

Do you prefer to home school your children?

If you are working right now, will you stay home after the birth of your children for three months, five years, or eighteen years?

Will you work part-time once your children attend school or not at all?

Will you work full-time and use daycare or hire at-home child care?

Will you bring your office into the home?

Will you begin to search now for a job situation that fits well with your lifestyle and values?

Does your husband hold similar views about staying at home once you become a mom and about who will bear the financial load, child care, etc.?

I don't believe that every woman is required by God to get married, have babies, stay at home, and stay in lower profile positions than her husband. But if you *do* choose to marry and have children, you must be willing to accept the change of focus in your life. You will need to take the focus off of you and your career and put it onto the family. How it all fits in from there becomes a matter of conscience, economics, convictions, and commitment.

Timing Is Everything

I would not be honest if I did not admit that I *often* struggled with the timing of pursuing my dreams and achieving my personal goals, but early on I determined that my dreams would not be achieved at the expense of my child. At each opportunity to take a new job, get a raise, move, or tackle a big project, my husband and I would sift these decisions on the basis of our priorities:

First, God: What would God's perspective be in this situation? Is this a wise move? Does it show integrity? Has God been leading us in this direction? Is this impulsive?

Second, family: How will each member of our family be affected by this decision? Will any of us be without the amount of love and nurturing that we need to be emotionally and physically healthy?

Third, work, vocation, and other considerations: What will this mean financially, practically, and relationally at work and to our budget? How will this affect time spent with our extended family? Will this affect our volunteer hours?

Having even one child has cost both of us time, money, and energy, all of which have been drained at various times to very low levels! Having a child has also meant that some of our dreams have been put on hold for a few—even many—years.

But an unspeakable joy and an immeasurable reservoir of love wells up in a parent every morning when you wake your child from a sound sleep, when he laughs out loud in his special way, when he says or does something especially cute, and as you watch him grow into a very special person with a terrific personality.

But your decision whether to have children should be made before you say, "I do."

Is There Such a Thing as a Traditional Woman?

In the days when a wife worked with her farmer husband, when both "mom and pop" tended the store, or when the wife "checked in" the patients for her doctor husband, what was considered "traditional" for a woman?

Perhaps in each era, each generation, a woman must find a balance within the economic times, her personal skills, family concerns, and location to define which roles in life she is meant to fulfill. Even as I read the passage that is considered to describe the "traditional" woman in Proverbs 31 with descriptions such as "she selects wool, works with eager hands, provides . . . considers a field and buys it, and sees her trading as profitable," I am inspired to think of this woman as an industrious, entrepreneurial, team-working, home-managing kind of gal!

I have to admit honestly that I struggle with the more traditional philosophy that says all women were *created* to stay at home with their children and be the domestic wife of their astute husbands. I personally believe this message discounts the fact that not all women have the same personality, desires, dreams, or destiny. In reality, not all women will marry, not all women will have children. And the issue of working moms in a nation where the economy has significantly changed is a strong consideration that simply must enter into the equation of why, where, and when a woman with a family works. Does that mean a woman has let go of family values or no longer fits the description of a helpmate? I don't think so. But it does mean spouses both need to help each other with housework, during big projects, and with child care!

In our home, we often eat out, we both cook, do laundry, and grocery shop—if we all want to eat healthy meals and wear clean clothes. In the Tirabassi home, we've opted for team-work, *because both of us* (before we met *and* for the past sixteen years of our marriage) have been "out there" trying to make a difference in our world. We see our teamwork as doubling the efforts of what only one of us could have done alone! And an added blessing has been more hours together as a family and even more recreational hours for my husband! (He's getting used to this arrangement—of more family time and less worka-holism—as are many men in similar non-traditional situations!)

Chapter Six

By Plan or Passion

We have all made choices. Some of our choices have caused suffering, both to ourselves and others. Sometimes we have chosen to sacrifice our own desires—when we knew this to be the right thing, and when we didn't understand the importance of insisting on what was best for us. Through it all, we have survived, and can now reap a harvest of wisdom from our experience.

The High-School Girl . . .

In one southern Ohio suburb a high-school girl got pregnant and decided to give her child up for adoption. She worked through a lawyer to have a part in choosing her child's adopted parents.

At the same time, in a northern Ohio suburb, lived a young couple who for eight years had struggled to have or adopt a child. After all the medical options had been exhausted and one adoption proceeding had fallen through prematurely, they continued, though discouraged, to hope for a child to love and nurture.

In October, a most unusual scenario unfolded at a women's convention. At the convention, a woman who was familiar with both the high-school girl's situation, as well as my friend's hope for a child! On the last night of the convention, the two women sat near each other, prompting them to discuss the incredible possibility of the upcoming adoption of this high-school girl's baby.

The couple wrote a letter to the young high-school girl, telling of their desires, lifestyle, and reasons for wanting to be the adopted parents of her child. The couple shared honestly how they longed to be parents but were personally unable to bear children. The couple gave the high-school girl the details of their own childhoods, including how the woman's sister had died on December 8, when as little children their house burned down in a fire.

On December 8 of that year, the high-school girl gave birth to a beautiful little girl. The couple's story in that letter became a sign to her that they should be the adopted parents of her little girl. One month after their adopted baby came home to live with them, the new mother became pregnant!

The Rape . . .

At the age of eighteen, Lee was raped by someone in her office building. This happened in the sixties, when you would never tell *anyone* something like that had happened. Previously a virgin, she became pregnant. Feeling that she had no other option than to carry this child to term, she moved to another state, found a couple who offered to take her into their home until she had the child, and gave the child up for adoption. Lee's life continued on though there remained a piece of her life that was missing. Eventually, she would marry a wonderful man and adopt his two children to be her own.

Over twenty years later, Lee answered the telephone to hear the voice of a young woman tell her that she was the daughter Lee had given up years earlier. The young woman wanted to know if they could meet—and if Lee would like to meet her grandchild!

Can you imagine meeting, for the first time, a daughter that looked just like you, who had a handsome husband and a beautiful daughter of her own? Lee's daughter also wanted to be sure that her mother knew of God's love and asked if she had met him personally. She had! Coincidence? Perhaps God's redemptive plan!

What greater good could have come from this situation than for Lee . . . Lee Ezell . . . to share her miracle born in tragedy through many books and a world-wide speaking ministry? She has been able to help thousands of women in similar situations, facing their broken dreams.

Fetus or Baby?

I received this letter tucked inside of a young couple's Christmas card . . .

> In August, David and I were surprised to learn that we would be parents in April 1994. So, we began plans for the life changing event. On December 3, the day before my thirtieth birthday, my water broke unexpectedly, and on December 6, Adam Charles was stillborn at 23 weeks (17 weeks early). David and I trust that God is in control of our lives, He doesn't make mistakes. We don't ask why, we just continue trusting. Adam is with Jesus now. We found that our faith in Jesus Christ has carried us through these

tough times, and our belief in the Scriptures gives us hope that one day we will be united again with Adam in heaven.

What a difficult time for them. What an incredibly courageous perspective of their loss. And what a powerful acknowledgment that the *life* of Adam began *for them* the day they learned they were going to be parents!

The Young and the Restless

Recently on an airplane I met a dynamic gentleman who held a very important position in the American music industry. Our discussions ranged from music to athletics to "the family."

Somehow we got onto the topic of choice. He felt *strongly* that abortion should be an easily accessible option for women. As we discussed the issue further, he admitted that twenty years ago he had paid for his girlfriend to get an abortion. He even knew the sex of the aborted baby. Up to that point in our discussion, he had been adamant about the freedom of choice. But when he mentioned his dead son, he became quiet.

Reflecting out loud he said, "I often look around at twenty-year-old young men and wonder where my son would be right now? What would he look like? Where would he have gone to college? What would he *be* like?"

When looking at his "freedom of choice" from that perspective, I sensed he had regrets about losing a relationship with his son, not ever having the opportunity to experience life together, for opting to terminate his little son's life before he ever had the chance to know him. There was nothing I could say to ease his pain or comfort his heart. He alone bore the consequences of his choice.

What all these stories have in common is that they show parents of all kinds dealing with the effects of their choices, whether good or bad, painful or joyful. The important thing to remember is that parenting should be a conscious choice. Even when it isn't, we are still responsible for choosing proper parenting attitudes.

The Chosen

I have done my fair share of struggling with having children. Before getting married, my husband and I discussed not having many or any children. I'm sure one consideration not to have children stemmed from some of my own negative childhood experiences. Having never felt very maternal, I was honestly afraid of the responsibilities of motherhood. I wondered if I would be too selfish or uncontrollably angry, . . . but mostly I was afraid that I would feel trapped and unhappy.

Another reason I was hesitant to have children was because of my strong entrepreneurial spirit. Though many women friends of mine looked forward to homemaking, child-raising, and a more traditional marriage arrangement, I never felt that way. As I look back on it now, I'm not certain if I was simply afraid of the commitment of time and energy that children take or understood too well my own destiny. Knowing that much of a child's early development is a mother's role, my husband and I realized early in our marriage that I could not juggle both a personal ministry/career and a lot of children. Therefore, together we made the decision to have only one child. Through almost seventeen years of marriage and sixteen years of parenthood, that mutual decision has been the best for all three of us.

Make a Choice

A woman *should* and does have a choice in childbearing. (Even the traditional Catholic woman is encouraged to make use of natural family planning.) If we made this choice *based* on its consequences, the seasons of our lives, and our sense of "call" or destiny, rather than out of selfishness, rebellion, deceit, or irresponsibility, our country would not be in the abortion dilemma it is in now.

It makes much more sense that truly intelligent, responsible women, who are deeply committed to their values and dreams, should determine their choices *before they enter into* relationships or positions that might change or alter the course of their lives. Even the woman who is surprised by love or unexpected life *in the process* of pursuing her goals and dreams still can make choices based on the responsibility of her actions and in light of her convictions.

In America, we all know that shooting a gun in anger, hitting a window with a brick to break into a building, or being married to more than one person are all *choices*, but all are self-centered, illegal, and harmful to other people. If a person *chooses* to commit any of those acts, he or she will also incur the consequences of their actions.

I believe that women *do* have *choices*. I also believe that the clear majority of women are intellectually capable of making those choices *before* a life is created or *before* a life has to be taken.

Take the Step of Premarital Counseling

Perhaps a preventative measure that would make the most sense in avoiding impulsive relationships and their many consequences would be for all pastors and priests to require premarital counseling as a condition in a prospective couple's plan for marriage. My husband, Roger, who is a pastor, will not marry a couple without premarital counseling. By using the excellent testing tools available today, both men and women are able to discover, *before* they marry, how they feel about children, sharing the housework, having one primary wage earner, or if they share similar religious or moral convictions. Premarital counseling, though not a one hundred percent guarantee of marital bliss, can anticipate most of the big surprises that can be hidden before a couple is married and can prevent *years* of frustration over unmet expectations. In essence, all the chips are on the table before "the game" is played!

Premarital counseling and testing, though not one hundred percent foolproof, will bring awareness to a woman like myself, who has an entrepreneurial spirit and lots of energy, of her need to gravitate toward a man who believes in the call in his wife's life—as well as his own. If anything, it should signal significant difference, encouraging a woman to be careful to date men who are not threatened, but delighted, by her successes!

After such counseling, the man who is attracted to that type of woman will be more apt and willing to share in the household chores and child care, not seeing it as woman's work but as a mutual responsibility.

For the woman who dreams of a traditional marriage—with a husband and large family—premarital counseling will confirm her match in a man who plans to be the main wage earner, has the capabilities and energy to do so, and desires a home *filled* with children, fresh baked goods, and home-spun memories!

Is either better? Is one more appropriate? I can only assume that every woman is an individual, created for her very own purpose in life. To presume that all women should do, be, and act the same as another makes no more sense than saying all men will marry, have three children, and work from nine to five at the office.

Ideally, responsibility for one's passions, one's definitions of marriage, and one's deepest desires should all be weighed heavily *before* marriage and children. If spouses would agree on their definition of marriage and family, then covenant with each other to be faithful, today's high rate of divorce and astronomical number of unplanned children might wound fewer innocent victims.

Men and women, whether single or married, don't have to go it alone. There is always someone else who knows the desires of their hearts.

Chapter Seven

Two-Way Conversations

As a child I learned to pray these words at bedtime.

> Now I lay me down to sleep,
> I pray the Lord my soul to keep,
> If I should die before I wake,
> I pray the Lord my soul to take.
> God bless Mommy, Daddy, Reggie, Ricky . . .

I panicked every time I prayed that prayer! I was only five years old! Was I going to die? How would it happen? Where would I go? (It didn't help that Grandpa, Grandma, and President Kennedy all died within a short period of time.) I thought their caskets were in my closet at night. (Weird.) Many nights, I could not fall to sleep out of fear of death. Eventually I suppressed the fears. . . .

What I couldn't suppress was a spiritual hunger that arose out of my deep despondency in my early twenties. Millions have taken the next step that I took in an attempt to find God. We could no longer go on in our lives. My generation has been searching for God. Perhaps in our youth we were disillusioned with the hypocrisy of "the church" and "religion," but as adults we still long to know God, as well as the meaning and purpose of life! We have been as low as we could get, and we have had nowhere to turn, or look, but up. We called on God. We cried out to him in desperation. And we found him waiting. Those conversations are called prayer.

My simple prayer was, "God, help. I'm not gonna make it. I hate my life. I'm lost. Is this who I was meant to be? Help. I need help. I need your help. I'm ready to change. Come into my life. Take my hand. I can't do this alone."

That was the first time I had prayed as an adult. With all of my heart and soul, I expressed both my pain and shame. I let all of my emotions unravel, crying aloud and collapsing like a daughter falling into the arms of a loving, forgiving father. I prayed with hope, believing that only God could help me. And he did.

Prayer, My Conversations with God

From that point, prayer became a newfound source of strength, a resource for power, a place for me to connect with God in conversation. It was not rehearsed or memorized as were my childhood prayers. It was spontaneous, personal, re-leasing, revealing, relieving, comforting, and always resulted in an inexplicable peace.

I prayed about whether I should move, for a job to open up, for friends to understand my new faith, and for my family members to come to know God—to find him as a loving Friend and Father.

And because of the way God had picked me up and out of my addiction, I continued to have a childlike faith that caused me to believe that though I could not see him, he was listening, he would answer, and I could trust him.

Over time, I discovered that prayer is not telling God *what* you want him to do; it is *asking* him to intervene, open a door, change a circumstance, heal an illness, or bring relief. Those of us who have seen God do the unexpected, miraculous, and the impossible have *also* heard God say "no."

Author O. Hallesby helped me to understand this non-negotiable aspect of prayer. In the book *Prayer*, he says, "When God says 'yes,' it is because he loves us, and when God says 'no,' it is because he loves us." It has taken me time not only to understand but to accept the "asking" principle of prayer. Along with the belief that my God is just, fair, loving, and sovereign in all of his ways, comes the confidence to believe that I have a direct and uninterrupted access to God through prayer.

Making Time for God

Ten years ago, I came to the realization that if I didn't make time in my life for God, as I did for the many other important people and projects, I would again find myself spiritually hungry and navigating my daily life alone. So I very determinedly set aside one hour each day to talk to God in a tangible, visible way. I began to journal our daily conversations.

God's answers to my prayers ranged from miraculous to mysterious. The act of journaling my prayers and recording how God answered each of them became my greatest evidence that God listened and responded to both my smallest concerns and greatest needs.

If you are skeptical that the God of the Universe has the slightest bit of interest in you, record—in writing—your conversations with him! You will no longer credit events to coincidence, chance, or luck. No, instead, you will be faced with the reality that there is someone, not some thing or some force, but a Living Being, who loves you, sees you, cheers you on, pleads for you to come to him, and prepares the way for you. Written prayer becomes black-and-white proof of the power of *God and prayer.*

From those initial hours in prayer, I developed a prayer journal, called *My Partner Prayer Notebook.* This prayer journal has allowed many who have searched and struggled with prayer both to make time for it *and* find God through it. It has opened the doors and windows to heaven for those of us who have previously considered that our conversations with God were hitting the ceiling and going nowhere. Written prayer has provided us the eye-contact and focus that it takes to carry on a conversation with an invisible God, so as not to fall asleep, daydream, or become distracted by the many urgent interruptions in our daily lives.

Learning to Tell God I Love Him

Each day I begin praying by writing and paraphrasing—in long hand—those poetic but powerful prayers in the Book of Psalms. I call this my "Praise" section. How interesting it is to read the recorded prayers of those called "Psalmists," observing their confessions, fears, cries for help, pleading for rescue, and praises for their Creator! As I read through the whole Book of Psalms each month, I find each chapter mysteriously pertinent on a daily basis, almost always intimately representing my personal thoughts, feelings, and fears. I use their patterns to teach me how to express my deepest feelings of love for God, to God.

Here is a sample directly from my own journals of how I quote and then paraphrase the Psalms.

June 22, 1993

Psalm 24
"The earth is yours and everything and everyone in it! You established it. Who may ascend your holy hill? He who has clean hands and a pure heart and does not lift up his soul to an idol—"

Lord, my hands, are they clean? My heart—is it pure? Do I have idols?

"For this person will receive vindication and blessing from you, Lord . . ."
"You are strong and mighty, Lord. You are the King of glory!"

Psalm 25 (my paraphrased version)
"To You, O Lord, do I lift up my soul. In you, I do trust—I have no other.
Show me your ways, please teach me your paths. Guide me in your truths.
No one whose hope in you will ever be put to shame, show me your ways, O Lord . . .
My hope is in you all day long! I will remember your great mercy and love.
According to your love will you remember me?"

The "Praise" section of my prayer hour is my daily habit of telling God how great I think he is and to speak words of love and respect to him!

Confess It All

Next, I actually acknowledge where I am struggling by identifying my personal failings and any problems in my relationships. I call this my "Admit" section. Though it is often difficult to articulate one's faults to another person, I know that if *anyone* can help a person to change, God can.

To come to God with our shortcomings, lies, admissions, and problems is not to burden him, nor is it to inform the All-knowing God of something he doesn't already know about us. In admitting to our faults we *agree* with him about our need to change. We ask for correction and direction.

On any given day we might not like what we see and feel about ourselves. Through prayer we can surrender and relinquish those faults and ourselves to God.

Recently, I received a letter that made me think Paul—a business associate—had changed our agreement without notifying me. I went ballistic. I called him immediately and gave his secretary an angry message. He called back just as angry, because he felt I had accused him unfairly. It turned out that he had not received my fax about the matter two weeks earlier.

My "Admit" section that morning read like this.

June 2, 1994

Search me, O God, for I don't feel generous or kind or good or willing to compromise.

Please know my heart—somewhere it was right and pure and good. . . . Now I am struggling with relationships and power and prestige.

Test me and know my anxious thoughts, O Lord, and see any (how many?) offensive ways there are in me. And lead me in the way everlasting.

Here's the bottom line: I'm not happy with everybody—so what does that mean?

Lord, I am in "help" mode. I need help in my relationships and with my business/management style. I don't have patience for anyone or tolerance—and I'm not learning and I'm not changing. And the truth is, I'm struggling with all of it. I need your help.

I can't.

You can.

I'll let you.

I don't know what to do next.

Is my baggage too great? What is your solution? What do you desire of me? Please speak to me.

I want to be a Christian woman who is loved and respected, and has great integrity in all of my relationships.

Help me somehow learn to be a team player. I find it so difficult to trust people. I find it so much easier to expect a disappointment from others than to expect that they will be on my side, not abuse me, not ever want to hurt me. Why is that? I know I have been abused. I have felt pain. I have been held back. . . . Lord, I don't want to be held back anymore. So create in me a clean heart and pure motives and fuel my passion for life with your perspective.

O God, I love you for loving me. Somehow you deal with all if us in a win/win situation. You are fair and just and right. Your favor, your love, your nurturing of me have been so special, purposeful, personal, and powerful. O how I love you, Lord.

When I called Paul back, we had a great conversation. We apologized to each other, and a mutual respect was reinstituted in our relationship.

Other journal entries from my "Admit" section . . .

October 10, 1993

"Search me, O God, and know my heart. Test me and know my many anxious thoughts. See if there is any offensive way in me and lead me in the way everlasting."

Give me insights and discernment, O Lord, on how I can be all that I can be for you as a: wife, mom, writer, speaker, and friend.

Help me to trust first, worry less, to walk with you, to be empowered by you, to love others, to see your viewpoint, to be confident in my call, and expect the impossible!

Teach me to evangelize. . . . Give me words and wisdom beyond my years.

A Changed Heart

When I consider all the addictions I have overcome with God's help—alcohol, speed, uncontrolled sexual patterns, and a foul, filthy mouth—I am even more confident that he will give me the strength and courage I need to control my temper, to forgive those who have hurt me, and to love the unlovely. Through this confession process I never feel like a worm of a woman, but I do feel shame and sadness for hurting and disappointing him, others, and myself. My motivation to change comes from the desire not to hurt those I love. (Just for the record: You should keep your journal in a safe place, as others might find its contents too tempting to ignore. But be assured, if others know you are daily talking to God about your faults, they may also be tempted to give you ideas on what to add to your list!)

It's Okay to Ask

The next section of my Prayer Notebook is called, "Request." I seem to have no problem asking God for and about anything! Half of the time, I think he considers me quite a big dreamer, a wild thinker, even a bit radical, but he's a big God. If it is according to his will, nothing I can dream is too big for him to accomplish. In fact, in all the illustrations and miraculous stories in the Bible, most of God's leaders had to stretch themselves to believe the impossible, trusting in his power and intervention.

In the "Request" section of my notebook, I feel free to ask and dream, receive ideas, and brainstorm! I am fully aware that *asking* God is not *telling* God. And I am also convinced that God's answers of 'yes' and 'no' are for the absolute best in each situation, even if I don't understand why.

Recently, on my prayer list I asked God to bring along an opportunity for my husband to teach, using his giftedness in counseling to train others. After less than one month, I found it not coincidental, but God's plan, when Fuller Seminary, unsolicited, called to invite my husband to be an Adjunct Professor to teach Youth Ministry.

I have prayed about moving to another state, writing specific books, selling our house, even attending an event or a class that I could not afford *unless* God intervened in some specific way—and each time "wild things" would happen to bring about a solution or answer to each request.

Most recently, I was informed by my friends at Cleveland Youth For Christ that they had given my name to the Northeastern Ohio Billy Graham Crusade Committee to be a possible speaker for the June 1994 Crusade in Cleveland. I was excited and encouraged to think that they would even consider me, but the fact that I had lived in Cleveland for much of my life and that most of my extended family and many friends still lived there gave me more cause to hope that I would be invited to share my story. The initial response came back to the effect that the Billy Graham Committee had never heard of me!

I did the only thing one can do in a situation that is completely out of your ability to influence—PRAY! I even wrote to my prayer-team members, asking them to pray: "Well, I'm not surprised that the Billy Graham Committee has never heard of me, but God has! So, my prayer is . . . Lord, if you have planned (before all time?) that I should have this most unique opportunity in my own hometown to share my story about how you came into my life, would you please open the doors?"

About two weeks later, I got a call and a letter inviting me to speak at the June 9, 1994, Northeastern Ohio Billy Graham Crusade! What a thrill! What an honor! What an exciting answer to an "asking" prayer!

I have come to believe that the ideas that *don't go away* are the dreams that God has given me to dream. In fact, I am growing more and more confident that *he puts* them in my heart and mind. Every book I have written, every fitness video I have produced, and every appointment with someone who doesn't know me that I have undeservingly acquired, has first come from a documented conversation with God and in the form of a request to him!

In *My Partner Prayer Notebook*, I've asked God, sometimes pleaded with him, to open the doors, to go before me, to give me favor in the eyes of someone, to show me how to do something, and to make it possible for me to move forward with my dream or idea—and so often he does. Answer after answer fills the chapters of my first two books on prayer in my attempt to motivate others to consider the power available in prayer, to encourage them to see prayer as a two-way conversation, and to remind them that when asking of God, be specific, expectant, and willing to accept his answer, whether the answer is yes or no.

Though the "Request" section of my Prayer Notebook is the most exciting part of my prayer life, my hour in prayer does not stop there. In fact, I write a hand-written Thank You note to God everyday, which follows in the "Thanks" section of my notebook.

On Thanksgiving morning, I wrote . . .

Thank you Lord for my . . .

T . . . irabassi family name; beginning with Roger

H . . . ome (we finally found one in 1993 after a year long search)

A . . . ssistant—Carissa

N . . . ever being without You!

K . . . eziah—our little girl puppy

S . . . on Jake—who is most wonderful and fun

G . . . iving to those who need it

I . . . ncome

V . . . ideo #2—*Thoroughly Fit* and its devotional!

I . . . nvesting in the future . . . finally!

N . . . eighbors, church family, friends

G . . . race . . . undeserved, but generously given by you.

Hearing God Speak

The second half of *My Partner Prayer Notebook* has five sections in which I record God's thoughts, ideas, perspectives, and messages to me. I am convinced that knowing God's will and hearing his voice are not disciplines that were meant to be magical or mystical.

I have experienced that knowing God's voice comes with practice and over time. As with any friends, the more time we spend together, the quicker we recognize their particular way of greeting us or saying good-bye. We become familiar with their sense of humor, more serious tones, even their expressions of anger. So I have found it to be with God. His voice is not necessarily audible, but it is inwardly present. It is gentle, but firm. I know when I am being corrected.

September 24, 1993

O Miss Becky, I love you. I show my love to you through Roger. Would you like to show your love to Me by loving Roger? What would it look like? Serving him, meeting his needs, thinking about what would make him happy and doing it:

- planning meals
- turning the light off first
- studying with Jake
- going with him to Lifelines (his high school group)
- hugging, touching, building up his self-esteem

Miss Becky, Tell the world of my love . . . write as a woman called to call all women unto me.

After a difficult business situation . . .

September 25, 1993

O Miss Becky, you handled Carissa's bad news with an extra measure of my Holy Spirit. Do you realize it is there for you to draw upon at all times, in all days? I love you, Miss Becky. My ways are higher than your ways. Be ever encouraged! I am going to do something in your day that you would not believe, even if you were told—though it lingers, wait for it. It will certainly come and not delay! It will, Miss Becky!

. . . and I responded with . . .

Lord, I sense you are stretching me, growing me . . . dealing well with me! Oh how I love you!!

I mostly hear his voice and sense his presence through my regular Bible readings. But in addition, the Holy Spirit's comfort and convictions, the teachings of pastors and teachers, and even circumstances are other ways that I sense God uses to confirm, nudge, or impress me to make a decision or a move.

My attitude is to wait expectantly for him to speak to me in any of the above forms of communication. As it says in

Psalm 5:3: "I lay my requests before you and I wait in expectation!"

In the "Listening" section, I quiet myself long enough *not* to talk. I listen and write down any thoughts or Scriptures that come to my mind during that planned time of meditation. On February 27, 1994, I wrote . . .

> Have I not shown you over and over, that it is not princes or men that will save you, it is I, the Lord your God, the Almighty God? Miss Becky—pray to me THEN, trust me to show you that I have heard you, will respond to you, that I go ahead of you and behind you.

In the "Message" section, I record the insights I gain during the times and opportunities when I hear a speaker or teacher communicate about God.

For example, after reading the daily entry in my *In Touch* magazine, I wrote . . .

January 8, 1994

Thank you for Charles Stanley's words,

- "a conquering faith rejects discouraging thoughts and words."
- "a conquering faith recognizes the true nature of the battle."
- "a conquering faith relies upon the power of God for victory."

Thank you, Lord.

Those written reminders daily serve to teach, inspire, touch, and motivate me.

In addition, I have made it a part of my daily spiritual growth to read a planned portion of the New and Old Testaments and Proverbs by paraphrasing or underlining a few verses that stand out to comfort, direct, or even convict me.

For instance, my journal entry for August 31, 1993 reads . . .

Proverbs 31
What does a wife of noble character look like?

- she is worth a lot
- her husband has full confidence in her
- she brings him good
- she selects
- she works with eager hands
- she travels far to bring supplies for her family
- she's an early riser
- she's a saleswoman, buying and selling property
- she's a wise business person
- she is a vigorous, strong worker
- her trading is profitable
- she works until late
- she is generous to the poor
- she clothes her family very well
- she is clothed in fine cloth
- she makes and sells and supplies (an entrepreneur?)
- she is clothed with strength and dignity so that she can laugh at the days to come
- she speaks with wisdom and faithful instruction

The Word, A Familiar Voice

My familiarity with the voice of God as I read the Bible deepens over time. Often, while reading a Psalm that includes the name, "Jacob," I sense God's personal touch, as Jacob is my grandfather's, father's, and son's name. I feel this name is my heritage as well. Psalm 46 is one of the chapters I have highlighted, as it says twice, "The Lord Almighty is with us; the God of Jacob is our fortress."

When I am praying about how to make a certain decision, I allow Scripture verses to cancel, confirm, or counsel me in the direction in which my thoughts and circumstances are leading me. The stability and consistency of the Word in my life increases my confidence to make decisions, to venture out into the unknown, or to trust God for the unusual, impossible, and difficult circumstances in my life.

And though I don't base a decision solely on one verse or passage of Scripture that I have read, I use my daily, regular Bible readings to prompt me in one direction or another. Psalm 119 refers to the Word of God in our lives as a light to illumine the paths we are to take. It even speaks to those who are young, encouraging them to allow the wisdom and authority of God's word to be their guide and counselor!

The Perks of Prayer

I have to admit, *one* of the reasons I am such a committed follower of the guidelines set forth in the Bible is for its benefits! Over time and after much rebelliousness, I've concluded that God's ways *are* what I really desire for my life. Repeatedly the Word has proven to protect, direct, and correct me, even teach me about the freedom that comes with discipline.

My pattern for prayer—my part and God's part—completes my two-way written conversations with God. Though I can't see him, because of the direct responses I receive to my written prayers, I am conscious that his hand is moving on my behalf. I am convinced that God hears my prayers, and as I've mentioned over and over, he continually surprises me with his answers.

Prayer, My Hiding Place

For many people, there comes a point of belief that God *is* the Creator of our lives and that he has a definite handle on time and eternity. Though we can guess, hope, assume, and estimate, we simply cannot manipulate, know, or see the future as God can. When we acknowledge God's sovereignty by surrendering our lives to him and then relinquish our vain attempts at control—one day at a time—we experience a deep peace.

Through prayer we have a safe—very safe—place of refuge, hiding, and retreat. In the inevitable storms and trials we encounter in life—and for most of us, there will be many—we can find our hiding place when and where we meet with God in prayer.

There is no safer place or person in whom one can confide than in the loving, living being known as God. But we must be honest with him. In moments of honest reflection we accept correction and receive motivation for change. This gains us access to God. When we become transparent with God, we actually feel his presence.

In prayer, we know—are assured—that failure is not the end of our relationship with God. In fact, we may find that he is the only one who will not and does not reject us in our failures, but that he alone can be trusted to open his arms out to us.

To Know God Is to Love Him

Sadly, many Americans see God as legalistic, powerful, and angry. I believe this misconception is emphasized, even proselytized by those who simply aren't *familiar* with the personal God of the Bible, causing many to turn from him before ever meeting him.

I am convinced that it is God's love that ultimately draws us to him. In my own experience, I know of no other's love that has been so completely unconditional and undeserved. I will never forget how he loved me in my worst moments. Today, I believe that he truly loves me just as I am. This gives me an even greater confidence that he will love me for whomever I become.

Prayer, My Privilege

In the beginning, praying consistently may take effort, even feel like a duty, but the more we pray, the more we find we want to. In my own meditative style I envision the One I call "Lord" (and somehow he does have long hair and a white robe) always walking alongside of me. I can almost feel him gently nudging me when he wants to get my attention by bringing a thought to my mind of something that I should write down; then I do! I can almost feel his arms calming me when I am anxious. I imagine his smile as gentle, kind, endless. He is my constant companion. He is always accessible, never too busy, never out of reach.

Because my spiritual hunger is constant and deep, I have decided that the only way to fill and fuel it is to spend time with God. Because I am so dependent on his love, counsel, affirmation, and comfort, I have purposed to talk daily with him by journaling, then listening to him by reading his word, the Bible. The outcome has been a pattern of two-way conversations that has absolutely affected every area of my life: motherhood, marriage, and ministry.

By spending time with God, I allow his wisdom to influence me, as would the counsel of a wise Father. When he surprises me with serendipities that *he alone* knows will make me happy, I am reminded that he is an interested and involved-in-my-life Father. I sense that he expects the best of me, as would a proud and doting Father. And because of who *he* is, I am motivated to please him, as well as show him and others of my love for him. I feel proud and privileged to be his daughter. And so I pray . . .

> *March 8, 1994*
>
> O God, you have given me faith to believe in the impossible. You have given me love enough to blossom. . . . I love you, Lord! I have a great need to be all that I can be for you!! I want to please you—in my home, in my family, in my ministry; in all of my relationships.

Tried and Tested

My hours with God have given me self-respect, strength to remain sober, courage to forgive, and hope in his power to change circumstances. As much as I love to talk, and as excited as I get about the adventure and the "unexpected" and surprises, I'd be crazy not to pray.

I have found—and tested—that spending time with God naturally leads to a biblical lifestyle that is marked by a reservoir of peace in stressful times, the will to live honestly with others, to remain faithful to my husband, to be responsible as a parent, and to teach my son the morals and values outlined in the Bible.

Prayer has been the place where I have identified my life purpose and has given me a much greater degree of personal discipline.

Chapter Eight

Fit, Forty, and Full of Faith

The Elusive, Perpetual, Endless Pursuit for Physical Fitness!

Through the first thirty years of my life, I fought to keep my weight down, to eat a healthy diet, and to like myself. At times I might have had success with one area, such as fitness, family priorities, or growing in my faith, but I never found success in balancing all the areas of my life as a woman *until* my spiritual life was established as my most important priority. At that juncture, I was able to put the rest of my life in order. By making time for regular exercise in my weekly schedule and being careful not to over-exercise, I maintained a sense of emotional peace, not just physical discipline. At the same time, I grew committed to eating moderate, low-fat foods, without growing obsessed with under- or overeating. I was no longer seduced by the quick-fix, crazy, fad, and yo-yo dieting regimes that never got the job done over the long haul anyway. And I grew comfortable with maintaining a weight that was healthy for me, one that was achievable without starving yet still eliminated those pinchable rolls around my waist! At last—long last—I had a decent relationship with food: I liked to eat, rather than looovvved (or lived) to eat.

Stepping Into Fitness

Over the past ten years, aerobics has been the key to my fitness program because it includes two of my favorite motivators—dance and music! But shortly after attending aerobics classes and exercising to home videos, I found myself wanting to be the teacher rather than the student! As soon as an opportunity arose, I auditioned to be an instructor in a local Southern California health club. A bit out of my league, I found teaching aerobics wasn't as easy as I thought, but this forced me to get to class on time, allowed me to create choreography, and choose my favorite motown music, and it kept me committed to three workouts a week—the minimum I need to maintain my goal weight.

After five years of teaching aerobics, I realized that very few classes or home fitness videos were performed to entirely Christian music. My idea to produce a video turned into a desire to fill a need for myself and the many others I assumed would enjoy the combination of a fitness industry standard workout and great Christian "rhythm and blues," hip-hop music. My hunch was right, and though the process of producing such a video took almost two years, the final result, *Step Into Fitness*, was reviewed and rated in *Shape* magazine as one of the top nine videos of 1992.

Imagine my excitement when my choreographer, Candice Copeland-Brooks, called to tell me the great news of the review *and* that I could find my photo in the magazine sandwiched between Jane Fonda and Judy Misset Shepherd, founder of Jazzercize! I was truly amazed that someone like myself, who had always been searching for the final fitness solution, could find her solution not only by being physically fit, but in becoming *thoroughly* fit—physically, mentally, emotionally, and spiritually!

Making the first video really was fun and very challenging. The greatest benefits for me occurred as Candice and I grew in friendship through the hours she spent teaching me choreography, as well as in sharing our spiritual lives. Recognizing our similar multifaceted roles as women, we developed a motivational devotional as a companion to my second step aerobics video, both called *Thoroughly Fit*. Having met so many others in our travels who also desired to lead and live balanced lives, we designed this tool to help others make necessary, but often difficult, lifestyle changes throughout a ninety-day period.

Setting Goals, Achieving Results

Over the past ten years—most certainly not overnight—I have learned to set goals, adjust and evaluate my workout schedule based on my family and work commitments, find variety in my exercise regime by cross training (including stationary and outdoor biking, stepping and power walking), become accountable to a workout partner, join a support group whenever possible, accept my uniquely inherited traits—and have back-up plans when the weather is bad, when my partner "no shows," or for the times I've lost interest in my regular routine.

But balancing the physical area of my life has not been found in exercise alone!

Low Fat and Non-Fat Equals No More Fat!

What I eat plays a big part in how I look and feel. Simple evaluation of my food choices revealed that some things just had to go! The most effective way I found to change my poor eating habits and turn them into healthier ones was to become more aware of what I was eating! Just by purchasing a "fat counter" and using it as my guide—until I became familiar with the fat content in most foods—I found I could eat at most restaurants, learn easy and healthier substitutions in exchange for what I used to eat, as well as eliminate the chore of calorie counting. For instance, just by not using butter on my breads, by eating less red meat, and very little fried foods, I was able to stop dieting! I loved my new choices of pasta with marinara sauce, salads, breads, non-fat yogurt, low-fat meats, and grilled or broiled foods. Even choosing the right foods during my heavy travel season was no longer a problem, once I knew *what* I could eat! And always in placing my orders, I add, "Could you please put 'this or that' on the side?"

Ideal Versus Realistic

Not one of us *really* believes in an ideal weight or look for *all* women, but we sure do act like it! We seem to regularly forget that (1) we can't change our genetic make-up, and (2) we must eventually accept our inherited traits! Liking ourselves for who we are and how we look continues to be the huge "self-image" obstacle for women in America.

At least as long as I've been around, our culture viewed fashion magazine and runway models, or the glamorous television and movie actresses, as the fitness ideals to which American women aspire. Those women are sometimes among the small (but fortunate) percentage who don't really have to work out to stay fit, women who were born with a beautiful complexion and a tiny waist and who have a stunning smile. Recently, in the January 1993 issues of *People* magazine and the book *Beauty and the Best* by Debra Evans, we learned of the many health hazards many of these women with their "ideal figures" actually run. These images of beauty are dangerous for those of us who are unhappy with who we are physically, who always find ourselves dissatisfied with how we look.

As a young woman I used to think if you were *not* skinny, blond, and beautiful, you were less important, less desirable, and would be less happy. I'm sure most women don't really *believe* that concept, but we struggle with it. Though we know that our outer appearance is only a small part of what makes us beautiful as women, we're also aware that it is big part of feeling good about ourselves.

Therefore, I believe that if we will just do the things that we *can* do to be in *our* best physical condition, our self-image and health will improve, and our feelings, attitudes, and actions toward others and theirs toward us will be positively affected! Though workouts and proper eating habits can't change our genetics, they can improve our physical fitness and appearance. Physical training alone cannot *free* us from the tendencies to be jealous or competitive. The fine line between a person's self-acceptance and their physical fitness blends together when one's focus is not on outer or "body" beauty, but on loving one's *whole* self—even with our genetic uniqueness—as God, who has made us, loves us!

As most of us will admit, if our physical area is out of balance—because of overeating, lack of exercise, or stress—everyone else will notice! Therefore, to make choices that move us toward a healthy heart and fit body will also make us happier, healthier, more helpful, and ultimately more balanced women.

When we look at ourselves as being whole persons, we realize that we are spiritual, emotional, and social, *as well as* physical. It is when all the areas of our lives are in balance that we will view our physical fitness as health-improvement, rather than an obsession with self-improvement, giving us time and energy to focus on other areas of our lives, such as our marriage, motherhood, and especially our mission!

Defining My Unique Design

Tapping into who we are, what we were put on this earth to do, and taking those God-implanted dreams that are in our hearts and minds and turning them into reality should be every woman's quest!

Because we are all individuals in our genetic make-up, temperament, and background, this "focus" area will be different for each of us. It might include

- pursuing career goals
- knowing where you want to volunteer your time
- being an entrepreneur
- home-schooling your children
- being a homemaker.

But for a woman, developing our unique gifts and talents will most naturally come in stages, depending upon our marital, student, or work status.

One of the best ways to discern what it is that makes you unique, what your are best at, and even what you *like* to do is to simply go to the local library or bookstore and check out a few books on the topics of Temperament Analysis, Personality

Testing, or Spiritual Gifts—books like *Please Understand Me* by David Kiersey and Marilyn Bates. Then read. And as you are reading, take notes on what feelings you have about certain illustrations, note additional resources and then begin to talk to your friends and family. Ask them, "What do you think I am good at? What have you seen me do well?" Then ask yourself those same questions and a few more: "What do I *like* to do? If I could do *anything* in my life, what would I do, especially if money or time was not an issue? What have I done that was successful in my life? What experiences were very fulfilling?" This is just the start.

It is never too late for any woman to formulate a mission statement! By searching, dreaming, asking questions, and taking tests to determine personality strengths and weaknesses, we become aware of our gifts and talents, as well as our long-term desires. We can then translate these results into a personal mission statement for our lives—one or two sentences that sum up who we want to be. Like a microscope being adjusted for clearer vision, our life purpose will slowly come into focus.

At forty, I'm still in the process of fulfilling my personal mission statement. I have determined that I am called to be a woman who is committed to communicating to others how to know God better; to make God known through the gifts that he has given me. As I look back over the years and at each of my job positions—from my teenage years to the present—I see how I have been perfectly prepared for the very work I am now doing!

When we define who we are, what we like to do, what our life purpose is, and how we could spend the rest of our lives achieving that purpose, *life itself* becomes an adventure, a journey, a road worth traveling!

Family And Friends

If we aren't careful, we women have the same tendencies as men to overwork and become overcommitted outside of the home. The result is personal fatigue and the temptation to ignore our special relationships!

To balance the social area of my life, I have had to make quality time with my family and friends a priority. Again, one significant procedure stands out as helping me remain firm in honoring my family time: saying no.

Saying no to many good opportunities, committee meetings, or even phone calls, and making sure to say yes to family time has been the key to taking my priorities from a wish list (or should list), and putting them on an "I will" list—meaning actual "dates" or appointments on my calendar.

I probably find this area easier to balance than most because I'm not a workaholic. I work hard, but play just as hard. I like to have fun, so I get my work done by a certain time so that I can enjoy a bike ride, a movie, or television show, even a vacation!

Again, I must point to my life ten years ago, when I made a decision to spend one hour a day in prayer. That discipline not only provided a spiritual center, but it also became the place where, in the words of Peter Marshall, former Chaplain of the United States Senate in the late 1940s, I get my "marching orders from the Captain." By daily discussing each detail of my life with God, then taking the time to listen to him speak to me (most often through my Bible reading), I feel more directed in my daily, weekly, monthly, and yearly "to dos."

For example, when I was a working mom in an office, instead of holding three meetings a week, I would hold one meeting and delegate responsibilities for the other two meetings. With my home office, instead of picking up the phone whenever it rings, I let the answering machine pick up the calls and schedule the return of those phone calls into my day, allowing me to proceed with the projects that have to be completed before my son comes home from school or by their deadlines. This eliminates the tempting distractions of lunch invitations, unplanned television-watching, or shopping jaunts.

In addition, I am not naturally disciplined, so every project or idea that comes into my head during my quiet time also needs organizing. The moment I get an idea, I write down whom I need to call or write, or what step I need to take next in pursing a goal, increasing my effectiveness of staying organized and saving time. (It does all seem to boil down to time, doesn't it?)

Learning to say no to what is not a top priority and yes only to the requests that fit into my personal mission statement—as determined by the season of my life as a wife, student, mom—has been one of the best skills I have learned, with many benefits to those around me, as well. Defining my priorities, commitments, and most important relationships—in advance—relieves the guilt when I firmly say no to good but distracting offers, and it gives me the confidence to say yes to family time, quiet time, and workouts. These priorities are regularly scheduled in my calendar.

Determining Stages and Defining Serenity in My Life

As a forty-year-old woman, do I work out and try to look, feel, and stay fit for others? No, I truly do it for myself.

As a working mom, do I sacrifice certain professional opportunities for less prestigious family commitments because it is traditional? No, I make those sacrifices because I truly believe it is the best for my *son's* self-esteem and growth and is ultimately pleasing to God.

Do I spend an hour in prayer each day because that is a discipline a "good Christian" is supposed to do? No, I spend time with God because I genuinely want to know him better and to be well prepared to make him known.

Why do I expend the time and energy to write and speak and create tools for others to know God better? I believe that I am called to pursue these goals and inwardly motivated to make a difference in my world.

What have I done to overcome the inevitable obsessions of womanhood and find balance in each area of my life? I am learning to accept what I cannot change and change what I can! (Sound familiar?) That universal serenity prayer actually comes from the theologian and martyr Dietrich Bonhoeffer:

God, grant me the serenity to accept the things I cannot change, the courage to change the things I can, and the wisdom to know the difference . . .

That prayer seems to fit most situations in a woman's fluctuating life. It brings a realistic perspective to life.

As women, we must look up—often, *always*—to find balance in the many different stages of our lives: adolescence, young adulthood, singleness, marriage, motherhood, in menopause, or in aging. Thank God! He is always there and he deeply cares!

As women who love God and recognize his power in our lives, it is our privilege to stand firm for what we believe.

Chapter Nine

You Should Never Swear at a Lady

I was catching a late afternoon flight. I had just completed an exciting business trip; I had shared my vision "to change the world" with those I thought could help me—and they seemed willing to do so! I felt as if nothing could burst my bubble!

Shuffling down the narrow plane aisle with two bags bouncing off my shoulders, I enthusiastically flopped down into my seat next to a well-groomed, well-dressed, "scotch on the rocks" kind of guy. He eyed me carefully, then asked, "Where are you going?"

"Back home to Orange County," I responded pleasantly. "So, what line of work are you in?"

He straightened up his tie and proudly admitted, "I'm a lawyer."

I can honestly say that I had never told a "lawyer" joke before that, but now I know why they're told! "Ohhhh," I replied, giving him the impression that I was impressed!

Then he asked me the fatal (for-those-who-aren't-really-ready-for-or-interested-in-my-answer) question, "So what do you do?"

"Well, I'm a Christian author, speaker, and aerobics instructor," I answered, smiling with confidence.

He looked perplexed. "So . . . what does a Christian author write about?" I could tell that he was not up for a huge debate; he was just looking for a brief sentence or two in response.

Quickly thinking how best to answer him, I attempted to cross over any bridges of misconception that might already be in his mind about Christians and said, "Well, I talk about having a relationship with God, rather than a religion."

"Hmmm . . . what do you mean? I attend church whenever I want to, and I believe in God. Isn't that 'religion'?" he pointed out, rather lawyerishly.

"Exactly," I said matter-of-factly.

I realized then that we were in for a bit of a discussion, so I continued with, "When I speak or write, I talk about Jesus as a personal friend and try to show the difference between someone who *knows* God versus one who knows all *about* God, but has never met him."

Either he had too many drinks by this point, or I had made him angry. He went ballistic on me. Within earshot of the other passengers around us, he erupted with a shout, "You're full of —! I don't respect you."

My mouth dropped open, my cheeks reddened, my stomach turned, and my eyes widened in shock! But with complete conviction I firmly and quietly said, while my eyes pierced his eyes, "That was rude. You should *never* swear at a lady."

He looked at me, seemingly taken by surprise that this thirty-some-year-old woman would rebuke his behavior. Not wanting another outburst to ensue, I added curtly, "I had planned to pray for an hour while on this flight. . . . Please excuse me while I read my Bible and write my prayers *in silence*." Purposefully, I placed earphones over my ears.

"Oh, so you're just going to shut me out?" he asked under his breath.

I didn't bother to answer him. I smiled smugly and proceeded to ignore him.

As I began furiously to journal my thoughts to God, expressing my intense feelings about this man, I actually noticed him looking over my shoulder! "Good," I thought, "I hope he gets an eyeful." But soon I became preoccupied in my journaling and proceeded to have my daily two-way conversation with God.

At the hour's end, I removed my earphones, capped my pen, and closed my Bible and journal, only to hear him ask politely, sincerely, "What pain could you have experienced in your life that you would pray and read your Bible for one hour a day?"

I turned my head so that I could look him square in the eyes and answered, "This is what I was trying to tell you earlier. I have a relationship with God, not a religion. I don't pray out of pain or duty. I pray to God because of who he is to me. When I was a teenager, I became an alcoholic . . ." I lowered my eyes to glance at the scotch he had been regularly refilling during the flight.

He immediately caught my thought and said, "I drink quite a bit."

"I can tell," I smiled. "I was one of those cheerleaders," I continued, "who drank and partied to have fun and to be popular. But alcoholism runs in my family. By the age of seventeen, I left home and began to do everything you tell yourself (when you're younger) that you'll never do—get drunk, smoke dope, be loose. Though in the beginning alcohol made my life exciting and fun, it wasn't long before it blurred my vision, stole my

dreams, and turned on me. In addition to becoming an alcoholic, I eventually became a drug addict and speed freak. At
that point I moved in with my California boyfriend."

He raised his eyebrows, as the story seemed to be getting
more interesting. As I imagined his improper thoughts, the
painful humiliation of that time in my life caused tears to
stream down my cheeks.

He presumed that his inquisitive personality and superior
professional skills had drawn me to this point of confession.
"I'm really good at this," he said.

I wanted both to scream and change my seat, but felt that
because I had gone this far, I would continue to tell him my
story—not because I liked this man, but because I wanted him
truly to *understand* my love for and devotion to God.

I lowered my voice as I continued my story, "I 'hit bottom'
with my drugs and drinking when I woke up one morning in a
bed next to someone I barely knew. In that very hour, incredibly disgusted by my own promiscuity and drunkenness, I admitted to myself that I was an alcoholic. It took only three
weeks for my withdrawals to turn into thoughts of suicide.
That day my whole life changed. At a court deposition for a
previous drunken driving charge, I emotionally fell apart, left
the hearing, and drove to a church.

"At this little church, the person I found to talk to was the
janitor, whom I had met when I had attended the Christmas
and Easter services that year. He seemed as if he had been waiting for me to return. Seeing how distraught I was, he told me
that I could become a brand new person if I would just say a
prayer to ask Jesus Christ to come into my life. I prayed his little prayer that day, asking Jesus to take control of my out-of-
control life.

"When I drove away from that church, I knew I had experienced something supernatural. I no longer had the relentless

thought that I must have a drink. I could articulate in my own words that Jesus had *literally* 'saved me.' I believed that he had saved me from drugs, alcohol, and suicide. I actually felt as if a new life had been breathed into me. I knew that he had given me a fresh start, a second chance that I didn't deserve. And the janitor told me I had been given the free gift of eternal life *just because I believed!*"

To my new lawyer friend, I said, "*That's* why I pray for an hour a day. I want to talk with God, to listen to him, to be near him . . ."

The lawyer was solemn and quiet. "Now I understand what you mean when you talk about having a relationship with God. Do you think I could have one of those books you write?"

No, I thought sarcastically to myself, but I quickly reconsidered. "Sure . . ."

"Here, let me pay you," he said as he reached for his wallet. "I'm afraid if I don't pay you, you won't send me your book."

Because he had really ticked me off, again I had to persuade myself to be friendly. "No, I'll send you my book . . ."

We ended the trip on a congenial note, and on Monday, I sent him my book *Wild Things Happen When I Pray*. Within the week, I received a fax thanking me for the book and expressing his wish that we stay in touch.

In the end, the lawyer retracted his words. He not only respected me, but he had the courage to tell me so . . .

A Woman in the Nineties Stands Firm

My lawyer friend was not the first person I have come up against who has chided, ridiculed, and sworn at me for what I believe. But I am convinced that a woman who desires to make a difference in this world must be willing to stand up to anyone

—even though it may not be easy or popular—for what she believes to be true and good and right.

That is why it seems so important that the convictions behind one's beliefs must be founded on something secure—so that when the pressure and power struggle comes, you can stand. For me to address the issues of morality, fidelity, and love with those who have different convictions certainly has been a test. But I believe that the reason I am confident in my beliefs and convictions is because they are based on the Bible, of which I am neither ashamed or embarrassed. I have great peace and inner security in knowing that I am not defending *my* premises or ideas, but confidently relaying God's prescriptives for a person's life.

When I'm pushed and shoved to waiver or worry, to bend and change because of the trends or times, I have only to remind myself that God's Word was written to give direction, protection, and hope, and to promote a peace-filled lifestyle. Because I am convinced the Bible's precepts bring us into the fullness of life, I become willing to follow—even yield my desires to—God's timeless set of values.

Does an angry or abusive person like that have the ability to hurt my feelings? Yes. Could he embarrass me? Perhaps. Can he cause me to waiver in my convictions? No. I don't answer to him.

Speak the Truth in Love

I am convinced that my greatest assets when speaking with someone who challenges me are to be well-read and to speak the truth in love. I will never back down from someone who is simply trying to intimidate me. Ultimately, my standards draw the line for me in making lifestyle choices and decisions in difficult situations. They give me the determination to refrain from swearing, lying, cheating, or hating. They give me the courage to abstain from drugs and alcohol, even if and when I am cajoled, made to feel embarrassed, or am encouraged to join in and participate. And as a married woman, the standards to which I am committed strengthen my promise to remain faithful to my spouse until death parts us.

A woman who stands for what she believes will not always find her beliefs popular; expressing these beliefs may also not be in what appears to be her immediate best interests; her convictions guide her decisions even in the most difficult circumstances, and this ultimately brings with it a tremendous freedom.

When we are inwardly motivated by timeless standards, we become outwardly committed to give to others, lead with integrity, and use our resources to make a difference in our world. I believe those are the characteristics that define powerful women.

Women with a purpose and women of passion.

Chapter Ten

Our Purpose, Our Passion

Recently, my friend Wendy and I were taking a long walk through the streets of the neighborhood where we had played giant "kick the can" games as children. These were the streets where, as teenagers, we had "cruised" in our parents' cars after school, day after day, cigarettes in hand, music blaring. Then as young moms, our children played together on these same streets until I moved to California.

This year I would be thirty-nine and Wendy would be forty. We had been neighborhood friends since childhood, though in elementary school had grown apart. Wendy had gone to Catholic school and I had gone to public school. In junior high and high school we "partied" together. In our twenties, as young brides and mothers we "worked out" together, once again living only a few streets apart. Now we lived thousands of miles apart, although for the past eight years we enjoyed the unique privilege of seeing each other three or four times a year, and we talked on the phone each month.

This particular morning as we walked—for exercise, of course—we also laughed, reminisced, and shared moments of silence as the memories of those years on those streets flooded back.

As we turned the corner, Wendy shared for the hundredth time how she continued to struggle inwardly with a relentless tension and frustration that welled up within her whenever she remembered attending Catholic elementary school. She had often shared how it had been unusually strict, but not in ways that made sense to a child. She seemed puzzled by rules that seemed to wound a child's spirit, rather than encourage, build up, or educate her.

As an elementary student, she vividly remembered being handed a report card by a priest and taking it with the wrong hand. In harsh words, this godlike figure in her life rebuked her and asked the class "Who takes a report with the wrong hand?"

The class responded in unison, "A dumb person." Wendy's punishment was to kneel in the corner for forty-five minutes.

In sixth grade, when the issues of sex entered into class discussion, the tone and mood of the class became laden with guilt and shame. She remembers her class being adamantly instructed to have sex only within the bonds of marriage and for the purpose—the sole purpose—of procreation! Again a priest intimidated his youngsters with the statement, "Anyone who has sex before marriage will go to hell. That means you . . . you . . . you . . . ," admonishing them with a random pointing of his finger.

We had rehashed these stories dozens of times. Always I asked, "Did anyone hurt or abuse you?"

"No, not physically, but emotionally and spiritually." Although her pain was not physical, it was real to Wendy. We wondered how the pain of those memories could still seem so vivid thirty years later.

As we walked, Wendy continued, "I recently attended a workshop where childhood situations, such as mine, were discussed." She described the new techniques she had learned for managing the emotional pain, forgiving the offenders and moving on . . .

As we turned the last corner toward home, Wendy thoughtfully commented, "It is incredible how much power the memories of our past have in our lives!" Then it hit us. Why had it taken us so long to see, so many years to find some *good* purpose in all of this pain?

For the past sixteen years, Wendy had been a Catholic school teacher. For the past eight years, she had taught in the very school she had attended as a child. Wendy had never articulated before what caused or propelled her to teach in a setting she had found so difficult to bear as a child, or why she would work in a system that paid so much less than the public school system. But on this particular Saturday morning, her reasons seemed clear. Wendy had been on a mission. She had been given a "ministry" to sixteen years worth of Catholic school children whom she had taught. All these years she had been fulfilling the purpose in her life—to be a teacher/role model who loved, nurtured, and built self-esteem in her behavioral disordered and third grade students—*in a Catholic school*. And she was good at it.

Fulfilling Our Call

Perhaps that is the way it is for many of us. Our passion
and purpose in life are born out of an injustice that we experienced or a lie that we lived with, an abuse we survived, an addiction that we overcame, or even a crime that we knowingly
committed. And out of the depths of despair, we look up to find
life's answers and solutions. Through our pain we discover our
purpose in life and are given the passion (and compassion) to
fulfill it. Because of our pasts, we find even greater meaning as
we go back to help those we know are trapped, lost victims.
Some of us even spend our whole lives throwing ropes and life
preservers, desperately pulling them to freedom! This has been
my experience.

We find our personal mission—our purpose in life—as we
come to understand who we are, where we've been, and where
we dream of going. We begin to identify our "cause" when a
desire to fight for that cause comes from deep within our spirit,
giving us courage to step out, even into the unknown. And we
discover how to fulfill our purpose as we open our minds to the
creative ideas that come from God, who gives us step-by-step
plans to turn our dreams into reality. Then at some sweet point
in the process and pursuit of our life's purpose, we acknowledge
that *before all time* we were created for this very "work" which
satisfies our soul.

For the past twenty-five years, my life has revolved around
either *being* a struggling teenager or helping teenagers who
were struggling! As my generation (and the next) faced drugs,
alcohol, and a sexual revolution, we became "escape-from-re-
ality" artists—myself being one of the most resolute escapees,
until I hit bottom!

Hitting bottom became my turning point. Because I could
get no lower than I was, I was forced to look up and there I

found God. He was there for me and the dramatic and abrupt changes that I experienced because of our relationship—a new peace, a feeling of worth, and a sense of destiny—were just too good to keep to myself.

Within six weeks of my encounter with the living, loving God, I embarked on a mission that has not changed in eighteen years, with a passion that has never faded.

At that time, I would *never* have imagined myself in Christian work! I could have seen myself as an actress, an athlete, even a physical education teacher—but a Christian writer and speaker and aerobics-video presenter? It took my greatest weakness—alcoholism—to set me resoundingly on the course of my life's journey. My desire to help hurting kids came only after I had become one of those kids.

Between the ages of twenty-one and thirty-one, I worked with high school students in the midwest and on the west coast. During those ten years, I worked between twenty and forty hours every week leading small groups, coaching, teaching, and spending one-on-one time with students. The type of students that I worked with ranged from troubled to talented, from poor to wealthy. But all of these students had a few things in common: They dealt with poor self-images, had many questions about life and eternity, and all responded to a significant adult who would spend time talking with and listening to them.

Now when I ask myself why I would spend all those hours with so many students for so little financial reward, my answer seems obvious! I didn't want anyone to make the mistakes, feel the pain, reap the consequences I had to face as a young woman. I identified with those who grew up in dysfunctional families, led lives that were out of control, truly felt lost, and in real need of help.

And like many teenagers today, I *started out* with a fun personality, a healthy portion of athletic ability, as well as good grades. But between the lustful lure of promiscuity and an insatiable appetite for alcohol and drugs, I proceeded to lose all self-esteem, morality, goals, and decency. And by the age of seventeen, I had already become a directionless, insecure alcoholic and drug addict.

In retrospect, I feel very strongly that if *one* significant adult had invested some positive time in my life as a teenager, I *would* have latched on to their encouragement and support, finding the courage to make better lifestyle choices. Instead, I floundered until my conversion brought sobriety with it at the age of twenty-one.

Taking the "Good News" Back Home

Within months of my dramatic turnaround, I found myself in the assistant principal's office of my former high school. I told him that I wanted to help hurting teens. I had an incredibly strong desire to share my difficult experiences with others who were caught up in drugs, sex, and alcohol abuse. I told him that I was compelled—that I just *had*—to share with high schoolers the exciting new life I had found in Christ! He found it hard to believe that I was even the same person! (And admittedly, the "Christ" part scared him.) But I didn't go away. Over the next eight years, I served as the cheerleading coach (for as many as forty-eight cheerleaders a year) and Campus Life director in the very school where I had been an alcoholic cheerleader! Coincidence? No.

My passion and purpose caused me to take what I had been personally helped by—the Good News, that Jesus Christ loves us and has a plan for our lives, that he offers forgiveness of one's past, a fresh start for the present and the promise of eternal life with him in heaven after death—to whomever will listen.

Healing America's Youth

I am convinced that investing in the lives of young people is one of the major passions that must be revived in our country before the healing of America will come to pass. Those of us who can afford to, *need* to be giving more money to student programs, sharing our expertise and love, and giving quality time to our own *and* others' kids. We need to believe in young people, to encourage them, to meet them where they are—with their style of music and contemporary lingo.

It is time for every American, whether we have children or not, to *invest in* the lives of young people in a tangible way. How? Put yourself in their shoes. Ask yourself, "What would have helped me?" Put yourself in their communities and respond to their needs in the ways that would have made sense to you at that time. Do it on your own or join in with one of the hundreds of organizations that are already in place but need your resources of money, volunteer time, office space, or unused equipment to make a bigger difference!

Care for the kids of America—all the kids, any of the kids, just *one* of the kids in your community today—and America *will* be a better place, and your life will have purpose and meaning.

Take a Stand

In America, we daily have the opportunity to meet less fortunate, less skilled, and less intelligent people. To be a nation of people that protects, guards, encourages, loves, nurtures, teaches, and welcomes—even the unborn—is the noble premise on which our country was founded. But it is frighteningly apparent that our country is potentially becoming a nation of uncommitted, violent, self-centered, greedy, racially arrogant, and politically driven people. To disagree or refute such an accusation would be a futile waste of time. We need only look around. We only need to read the statistics that the United States is number one in violent crimes, alcoholism, drug abuse, abortion, and illiteracy in the industrialized world!

Now is the time for women who desire to live and act differently to make a move, to take a stand. As individuals, as women, as Americans, our country needs to be revived, renewed, rekindled, and returned to a nation that stands for what is good and right and true—under God.

We have the opportunity every day—if we will just look for it and be alert to it—to treat all men and women of all colors with respect, justice, and kindness. We have the power to value the lives of the elderly, handicapped, and unborn. We each have the responsibility—and most of us the resources—to help the needy, poor, homeless, and hungry.

We each can stand for, stand by, and stand with other Americans in their time of need or in their pain. And if no one has asked you yet, then take this as a request to . . .

Help the homeless by locating your nearest city mission.

Get out your checkbook, and write a check to organizations that help the hurting, such as Compassion, Samaritan's Purse, or World Vision.

Take a big plastic bag or box and fill it with those warm, but too small, clothes out of your closet. Then walk to the phone and call Goodwill or a local women and children's shelter.

If you are retired, call your local hospital or non-profit organization and offer to volunteer your time or expertise. And do it today.

Call your local high school, teen ranch, abused women's shelter, youth center, or church and find out if they need something—anything! See if you can fill the need! Go ahead. That's when we'll start to make a difference in this nation . . . when you and I get off our duffs and decide to stand for those who cannot—yet—stand for themselves!

As we do so, we will make clear what it means to be wild, wonderful women for God, and our voices will be heard and respected.

Chapter Eleven

I'm a Woman, Hear My Voice

Through the pages of this book, you have met and experienced an American woman who is a Christian seeking to be relevant to her culture. I would like to suggest that the *majority* of Christian women are like me. They are fun, faithful, fit, caring, active, moral, and productive contributors to the American society who have been unfortunately misinterpreted, misunderstood, maligned, and ridiculed. Partly because the secular media has been allowed to unfairly portray Christian women—and without serious rebuttal—I have written this book. Initially, it was born out of frustration, but by this time in my journey, I can simply say that I am proud to be a Christian woman. In fact, I believe that I represent the majority of Christian women in America who love God, love others, live to *spread* the Good News, and do not live to force other Americans to comply with our convictions and beliefs.

I would admit, though, that a good number of professing Christians have fallen short of their calling, hurting the reputation of all other Christians. Predictably, the least normal acting and looking, or the most hypocritical Christians, are the people the secular media present as typical.

Redefining Today's Christian Woman

When I define myself as a "Christian woman," I am referring to a deep faith in God that fuels my passion and purpose in life. I am also saying that I am driven by a set of values and convictions that I find in the Bible. These, having been tested over time, serve to guide me in the many daily and difficult decisions that I, as a woman, face.

As a Christian, I am compelled to love others because I have personally experienced an indescribable love and undeserved loyalty, when in my most broken and humiliating state, I invited Christ to come into my life as my much-needed Savior. On that day I accepted Christ's sacrifice as my passageway to God and received a second chance, a fresh start, a whole new life. With this act of my will, I became a Christian, a follower of Christ.

From that moment, I had a sense of destiny that comes from knowing and believing that God had a plan for my life even as I rested in my mother's womb. Because I put my faith in God, I no longer had to worry about dying. I had—and have—a peace about knowing that I will spend eternity with God; not because I have earned it, but because Jesus earned my salvation, paying the price for my sin that I might not be eternally separated from him, but receive eternal life as a free gift.

As a result of God's mercy toward me, my Christian life should be characterized by forgiveness of those who have hurt me because *I* have been forgiven *over and over*—and especially when I didn't deserve it.

As a married Christian woman, I also believe that I have a *responsibility* to be a faithful wife, honoring the decision I made in front of God, my family, and my friends on the day that I got married.

As a Christian woman, I am free to *choose*, but I base my choices not only on how these choices will affect me, but on how they will affect those I love, and those to whom I seek to be a role model and mentor.

And because I have been given talents and gifts, I am called and equipped to make a difference in my world for truth and good and God.

I must add that this Christian woman loves to laugh, dress nice, be happy, and squeeze as much fun that I can fit into any given day!

Does that sound like a dangerous Christian woman? Perhaps the most dangerous Christian woman of all—the person who is *real*.

Dangerous Misconceptions

For far too long the Christian woman has been misconceived as a . . .

> dangerous,
> doormat,
> dowdy-dressing,
> phobic,
> anti-everything,
> closed-minded,
> legalistic,
> serious,

poor,
isolated woman.

My perception of a Christian woman of the nineties is . . .

confident, not arrogant
assertive, not aggressive
spirit-led, not egocentric
determined, not stubborn
persistent, not pushy
fun, not flighty
friendly, not flirtatious
sexual, not sexy
fair, not prejudiced
encouraging, not jealous
generous, not selfish
beautiful, not boastful
fashionable, not frumpy
disciplined, not idle
special, not stereotypical
free, not addicted
gifted, not guilty
sacrificial, not greedy
committed, not fickle
ambitious, not power-hungry
a winner, not a loser
competitive, not cut-throat
an overcomer, not a victim.

I see Christian women as political "movers and shakers," volunteers, and activists. I see them spending time with younger women by teaching, leading, and impacting them for good and right and truth. I see them as women with families; both at-home moms, as well as working moms. They are women who choose, whenever feasible, to sacrifice their career advancement for the option of raising their children, and often later return to work outside of the home. The Christian women I know are productive, powerful, and passionate.

All women in America today—including Christian women—are redefining themselves. I believe that the Christian woman is *defined* by her relationships with God and others and her integrity.

Christian women are strong, not weak. They are able to sacrifice—whether it be in career or with money—simply because the attributes of a Christian (not just women) are humility, service, and surrender. They are industrious and talented. They are children of God and followers of Christ. They know how to love by decision, as well as emotion. They make a positive difference wherever they go—in schools, at work, or in the community. They are appealing. They know their weaknesses and will admit them, and work to change them. These women are not afraid to stand up for what they believe to be good and right and true. These women are valuable in America today. In fact, I believe we need more women who will identify themselves as "Christian" in America.

The Christian woman in America includes the single and the married, the working and the "at-home" mom. You will find her to be educated, skilled, and using her talents in her community. She is not afraid to lead, nor will she be held back from leading. She is able to fight diligently, but fairly, for a cause. She is willing to see the value within each person and rather than judging others, she will work for what is right to prevail.

It Is Time

For many years, I have dreamed and prayed that I could impact my country, as a writer and speaker, in the way that

Catherine Marshall, wife of Peter Marshall, former Chaplain of the United States Senate in the late 1940s, and later the wife of Leonard Lesourd, Editor of *Guideposts*, impacted her generation—with the relevance and power of an exciting, adventurous, appealing relationship with God.

I have not stopped hoping, dreaming, praying, or believing that faith in God could once again be relevant in America. I have not stopped praying for a genuine love for God to be revived in American men, women, and children. And with that hope, and to fulfill my dream, I have written this book.

It is time for Christian women in America to be heard, respected, and seen as wild, wonderful women for God. Will *you* be a wild, wonderful woman for God?

If you would like to contact Becky for more information about her books, videos, or speaking schedule, please write, call, or FAX

Becky Tirabassi
Box 9672
Newport Beach, CA 92658
1-800-444-6189